IN THE NAME
OF "PROGRESS"

IN THE NAME OF "PROGRESS"

THE LIBERALIZATION OF CHRISTIANITY

Christian Hartsock

iUniverse, Inc.
New York Lincoln Shanghai

IN THE NAME OF "PROGRESS"
THE LIBERALIZATION OF CHRISTIANITY

iUniverse books may be ordered through booksellers or by contacting:

iUniverse
2021 Pine Lake Road, Suite 100
Lincoln, NE 68512
www.iuniverse.com
1-800-Authors (1-800-288-4677)

ISBN: 978-0-595-42271-5 (pbk)
ISBN: 978-0-595-86608-3 (ebk)

Printed in the United States of America

"Your attitude should be the same as that of Christ Jesus:

Who, being in very nature God,
  did not consider equality with God
        something to be grasped,
but made himself nothing,
  taking the very nature of a servant,
  being made in human likeness,
And being found in appearance as a man,
  he humbled himself
  and became obedient to death—
    even death on a cross!
Therefore God exalted him to the highest
    place,
  and gave him the name that is above
    every name,
that at the name of Jesus every knee should
    bow,
  in heaven and on earth and under the
    earth,
and every tongue confess that Jesus Christ is
    Lord,
  to the glory of God the Father."

—Philippians 2:5-11

"We beg you to watch out for people who split up the family and cause brothers and sisters to take their eyes off Jesus. Keep people like that away from you because they're not serving Jesus. Their cool-sounding head trips are just going to snuff your relationship with Him. No matter how strong your trust is, you have to be ready to deal with people like that and yet keep your heads clear of their evil trips. And remember, the God of peace is going to smash Satan soon … Dig it!"

—*Letters to Street Christians*, by "Two Brothers from Berkeley," Zondervan Publishing House, 1971

CONTENTS

ACKNOWLEDGEMENTS

Before the book begins I want to express my gratitude to Gary and Vicky Hartsock (my parents); Ariana Hartsock (my sister); Mary Lou Weggenmann (my aunt and self-avowed "biggest fan") and her husband, Bob Weggenmann; Jake and Mary Ann Ariansen (my other aunt and uncle); my cousins—Janet and Patrick Nunan, Karen and Steve Gainer, Char and Kyle Gladden, Sonja Ariansen and Bret Ariansen; my grandmother, Viola Hartsock; Bob and Rachel Hartsock (my uncle and aunt on my dad's side); Alison Dahlstrom (who read through and critiqued many of the chapters right after I wrote them—at the risk of her employers at KFAX AM 1100 bursting into the office and catching her doing something non-work-related); and Robb Hedges (who has been an invaluable role model and unwitting moral and spiritual counselor to me for as long as I've known him).

I also want to thank my colleagues in the political commentary business who have been so supportive—Bruce Walker, Krystle Russin, Hans Zeiger, Marie Jon', Marvin Olasky; the editors who have consistently run my columns on their websites for the past couple years—Steve Stone at RenewAmerica.us, Frank Salvato at NewMediaJournal.us, Edward Daley at Times-Post.com, J.B. Williams at JB-Williams.com, Nathan Tabor at TheConservativeVoice.com, Greg Borse at Chronwatch.com, and the editors of a host of other magnificent websites including TheRealityCheck.org, IntellectualConservative.org, EtherZone.com, EnterStageRight.com and many, many others who know who they are. (I will be expecting a check in the mail from all of you that I just mentioned for promoting your websites.)

I also want to thank Judge Roy Moore for being one of the most inspiring human beings I have ever had the pleasure to meet, for granting Alison and myself that interview for our documentary, for welcoming us to his personal party, for the gratuitous fifty dollars he gave me for the cab ride back to the Montgomery airport, for being the main attraction of the most enjoyable trip I ever took, for being an inspiration and distant role model to me throughout high school, and, of course, for standing up for my religious rights as a Christian in

America at the expense of his job and reputation. He may not be governor of Alabama, but to me, he will always be my ideal appointee to a much higher position—Chief Justice of the Supreme Court of the United States of America. *That* is where a man like him belongs. Also I want to thank his public relations director, Jay Holland, who was a great friend to me and Alison, and who was kind enough to help arrange the interview with Judge Moore and on top of it—gave us a late-night tour of the beautiful Alabama State Capital and delivered us from a long, cold wait for a cab by giving us a lift back to our hotel.

I want to give a shout-out to the people in my churches, both in Nor-Cal and So-Cal: my homies from First Covenant Church in Oakland (a church that will always be in my heart and my prayers no matter what I have to say about it)—Pastor Paul Wilson, who helped finance my upcoming feature film and has been a wonderful beacon of support for everyone in the church; Mark "The Shark" Nielsen (the best thing Pixar's got going for it) for being the leader of my small group with Philip Goedinghaus and Matt Kanbergs since the days that preceded his work on *Monsters, Inc.*; Danny Fitelson, the high school youth group minister who was always down for a movie night; Marco Ambriz, an articulate pastor and valuable friend; and Pastor Emeritus Bryan Jeffery Leech, a wise and righteous man and fellow lover of films who always had a good Hitchcock film to show me. Also meriting shout-outs are my friends at Community Bible Church (CBC) in Ventura—Pastor Ron Blomberg, one of the most articulate and honest pastors I've known; Jim Lawhead, a welcoming and hospitable friend since I first started attending CBC, who played an integral role in my baptism as an adult; Joe Dilbeck, who has given me a lot of advice and support and also helped organize my baptism; and John Harrell, the college group leader, always a good speaker and listener.

Following this I would like to extend my limitless gratitude to my new fellowship at Emmanuel Evangelical Free Church in Burbank—a church more permeated with the Holy Ghost than any I have ever been acquainted with.

Of course I want to thank God, for pulling me out of the darkness and giving me a new life, for also giving me the heart of the artist—with which comes a greater perception of the world and the forces at work within it—a heart inexorably filled with excruciating pain and existential suffering but which also experiences seasons of indescribable joy that most people could never understand (unless they're on some good ecstasy). With this heart also came a voice, and it's that voice and the inspiration fueling it that I want to thank him for.

Finally, I would like to dedicate this book to the heroes of America, and all those pastors across the world who are acting responsibly in their positions—that is, not taking their positions for granted or using them as soapboxes from which to preach humanist values and not being so intimidated by the burgeoning cultural trends of the Swedes, the French, the Northern Californians and the Northeasterners that they find themselves censoring, sweetening, or pacifying the truth as written in the Gospels. These are the true heroes who are serving the world adequately in the name of God: our troops in Iraq and Afghanistan, our missionaries in the Eastern Hemisphere, and our ministers who count themselves dead to the world, alive with Christ, and inescapably responsible for the souls of those they preach the Word to.

INTRODUCTION
Beyond Conservatism

Ever since I was young I was always a voracious reader of books. You could never catch me at a time when I wasn't starting, finishing, or in the middle of a book. I rarely read required reading for school (much of it I had already read for pleasure). I spent all my time reading about my passions—film and politics. Be them biographies on Stanley Kubrick, Oliver Stone, Woody Allen, Marty Scorsese or Quentin Tarantino, histories of Communism, the Soviet Union, the Cold War, the Middle East, the United States or religion, or heated political commentaries by Ann Coulter, Bernie Goldberg, David Horowitz and radio talk show hosts Laura Ingraham, Michael Savage, Rush Limbaugh and Sean Hannity, I ravenously devoured them like Monica Lewinsky devoured—nevermind.

What I always couldn't stand about books, however, were the introductions. Yes, there always had to be not only a forward, but a forward and a preface, and not only a forward and a preface, but a forward, a preface and an introduction—and 129 pages later—voila—the book finally begins. And you can't skip these parts of the book because if you do you don't feel fulfilled. So as my revenge against the world for forcing me to endure those annoying pseudo-chapters that only serve to tediously delay the recompense for the $29.95 I spent on the damn thing (assuming the book was hardcover, which it usually was because I tended to buy them right when they came out), I'm going to make you suffer through this long and exhaustive introduction I've written purely for the sake of the sadistic satisfaction it provides me. Just kidding. I'll make it short.

For those of you who are unfamiliar with me or my work, I'll introduce myself. I'm a young filmmaker and political columnist, currently in college, whose work is routinely run on several websites, including RenewAmerica.us, Newsbull.com, NewMediaJournal.us, TheConservativeVoice.com, and others, including my own website, www.ChristianHartsock.com. I was born when Ronald Reagan was in his second term as president, and yes, I am, as Hans Zeiger (whom you will meet later in this book) would call me, one of "Reagan's children." This means that I am one of those insubordinate products of the disastrous baby boom generation who are too stubborn to adopt the baby boomer values we were supposed to inherit and pass on to the children of the next generation—that is the ones we don't abort as holy sacraments in the name of women's lib.

But don't get the wrong impression. I'm not one of those elegant, proper College Republicans or those fresh, young, affluent GOP poster boys who wear red ties and blue suits and American flag pins, clench their jaws and raise their chins and try to carry on Reagan's legacy to the dismay of those socialist, tax-and-spend Democrats. My politics were not spoon-fed to me by my parents (one of whom is an independent, the other of which is a McCain moderate who supports affirmative action and opposes the death penalty—except for Charles Manson).

If anything I take mostly after my grandfather, whom I never even got to meet because he died of lung cancer from smoking in 1958. Like myself, Jacob Ariansen was a strong Christian, a writer, and an uncompromising patriot—which would later get him in trouble. After coming to the States from Norway, my grandfather fell in love with America, and he founded, published, and wrote for a newspaper called the *East Bay News*. At one point in his career, he exposed in the paper the names of card-carrying members of the Communist Party he had met who had been working for Harry Bridges and the Longshoreman's Union. Because of this, he was beaten and left for dead. But that didn't stop him, which is why he was beaten and left for dead a second time thereafter. I have not been beaten and left for dead, but I am hated by many across the country because of the things I have written in my columns—and I will be hated even more for the things you are about to read.

While we're on the subject of my family, I might add that the reason I am here in this country is the same reason as to why I am bothering to write this book. My mother's maternal grandparents were Protestants from Greece who emigrated to America to practice and spread Protestantism freely without governmental persecution. My family had been persecuted by the Greek government for illegally preaching Protestantism (while the official state religion was Greek Orthodox), so we came here to the States to be persecuted by the ACLU. In the words of Pete Townshend, "Meet the new boss, same as the old boss."

In an attempt to repress my attention deficit disorder, I'll return to where I was before. Purple cherry blossoms floating over a thousand leagues of impudent snails, right? Just kidding. I might add that I didn't grow up in one of those red "fly-over" states that liberals always speak of in condescending sighs. (Although I do have a special affinity with Southerners and am very fond of the South—particularly Alabama. Many even say that I have something of a Southern drawl.) I grew up right next-door to Berkeley and right across the Bay from San Francisco (or as I call it: "the Brokeback Soviet Union"), so don't try to tell me I'm a conformist or a product of my environment. If I was, I would be wearing much tighter jeans, drinking a lot of mineral water, reading a lot of Chom*sss*ky, watching a lot of Bravo, pledging allegiance to the Rainbow Flag, I would have cried during *Rent,* I would have a bizarre, platonic fetish for Judy Garland and I would have a much better sense of fashion.

Yes, I am a conservative across the board; I'm a right-wing extremist and I admit it—unlike liberals, who are so taken aback when you call them "liberals" that they tear their shirts and threaten to rip out your eye-lashes and sue you. (Then they huff and puff and march back to their mothers' basements and try to cheer themselves up by fantasizing about having pillow fights with Fidel Castro and by watching their favorite episode of *Faces of Death*—the one with the uncensored footage of the partial-birth abortion and the sex change operation featured back-to-back.)

I am not your typical conservative. If you were to look into my past, you would not see the track record of a typical Christian conservative. Because of this, I can probably never run for office—especially as a Republican—so all you liberals can breathe a sigh of relief on that note. (But the fact that George W. Bush became president gives me *some* hope ...) I am a registered Republican, but I don't believe Republicans have all the answers or that their party is the answer to all the country's problems. I support George W. Bush, and he was the first president I ever voted for (he was lucky enough for me to turn eighteen a week before the 2004 election—you're *welcome*, George!), but I think he did a much better job in his first term.

I am a pragmatist: I am against third parties. I have always voted Republican, but I have sent out a threat to many of my fellow Republicans that I may cross the aisle if the 2008 Republican presidential nominee is who I think it very well could be. (I won't say who I'm talking about but I'll give you a hint: His name starts with a "John" and ends with a "McCain.") I was never into sports. I am only a Raider fan because I'm from Oakland and have a lot of Oakland pride. Frankly, I don't even know if they're a good team. What with Jay Leno's frequent derisive references to the Raiders in his monologues, I get the feeling they're not. To me, the Republican-vs.-Democrat game is the only sport I play. And I play it as if it were a sport. I'm passionate, I strategize, I always want to win—but my real battle is fought outside the coliseum.

As I will mention later in this book, (I hope you're beginning to understand the futility I see in introductions) my conservative politics are the moisture rings a glass of water leaves on a coffee table without a coaster. The water in the glass is my faith. Democrats raising taxes, illegal immigration, campaign finance reform—these are all civilian affairs. Let the College Republicans and the GOP poster boys with their red ties, blue suits and flag pins take care of those issues. I am not a civilian. I'm a soldier of Christ. My battle is not just against the Democrats who are screwing up America but against the scourge of liberalism that is screwing up the church. For years I have been an activist against the ACLU—standing up for the church against outside forces. But this book is about me standing up for the church against the liberal cultural termites that have infested it from within and spread their malignant microbes of self-described "progressivism" that is, yes, attracting many to the church, but leaving them with a neutered, accommodated, politically correct understanding of the religion that reserves so much room for "community," "diversity," and "tolerance" that there is no room for the way, the truth, and the life. There. You're now free to read my book with a sense of fulfillment.

—Christian Hartsock
Los Angeles, California
April 2007

CHAPTER 1

LIBERALISM DEFINED

Ironically, liberals have ecstatically promulgated the theory that Christianity has been hijacked by the "religious right" (this is assuming liberals ever had anything to do with Christianity in the first place). Essentially, this scenario is tantamount to a practicing homosexual accusing another man of stealing his girlfriend.

To liberals, the Christianity practiced by conservatives is a religion of intolerance, sexism, homophobia and warmongering, while the Christianity practiced by them is a religion of tolerance, diversity, peace, community, spirituality and Jimmy Carter. The question lingers: Why do liberals care so much about having something they clearly know nothing about "hijacked" from them?

We have read scores of columns (many mine) and books from David Limbaugh's *Persecution* to John Gibson's *The War on Christmas* observing the external assaults on the religion America's laws were predicated on, such as liberals' heroic stand-up against "religious nut" Judge Roy Moore and their wonderful tendencies to steal Bibles from small schoolchildren and throw them in the trash. I made a documentary with a young model and actress by the name of Alison Dahlstrom called *Separation,* which was an expose of the left's attacks on Christianity. What liberals have been getting away with more cunningly, however, has been their *internal* assault on Christianity.

Just as Soviet spies like Alger Hiss and Julius and Ethel Rosenberg (and the countless others listed in the Venona cables) tried to assimilate themselves to American culture so as to hide their true identities, liberals have swooped into the wading pools of Christianity and denounced the deep-sea divers who are only the way they are because they have fully submerged their souls into the depths of Christianity—a faith liberals feel they—*they*—have a true monopoly on.

And they have come up with brilliant—just *brilliant*—methods of pretending to know what Christianity is about, such as speaking in flowery, orgasmic tones about how *spiritual* they are (liberal atheists like to insist that while they may not

1

be religious, they are "very spiritual"), trying to convince us that God is a "she," (or worse:) that Jesus was a l-, Jesus was a llli-, (I give up) Jesus was a liberal, and that his primary purpose was to bring world peace.

A website called JesusIsALiberal.org cites scripture that is supposed to corner us into believing that Jesus was a tree-hugging, granola-eating liberal who opposed the death penalty—specifically Matthew 5:21, which reads: "Thou shall not kill." Now if they had used the proper translation it would have read, "Thou shall not *murder*" (emphasis mine). According to the American Heritage Dictionary (Third Edition), the term "murder" denotes: "The *unlawful* killing of one human being by another, esp. with premeditated malice" (emphasis mine again). Inasmuch as the death penalty is carried out by law (except in abortion clinics), it does not constitute *unlawful killing* and hence—"murder." Whoops! Guess they'll have to rethink that one.

If you want to know liberals' real agenda, just listen to "Imagine" by John Lennon (a song my high school U.S. history teacher bizarrely made my class sing along to). Their ideal utopia is a world where "there's no heaven," "nothing to kill or die for," "no possessions," and (most significantly) "no religion too." They believe such a utopia is possible. And this explains why liberals, being the sore losers that they are, to this day won't admit that Ronald Reagan defeated the Soviet Union.

The central reason for why liberals despise Christianity so much is because they are appalled by the worship of someone who is not one of them. Like Adolf Hitler, they don't believe in the sovereignty of God, they believe in the sovereignty of man. And this explains a lot. For instance, they think they have the right to terminate their own pregnancies because they are gods. They think that they have the right to redefine a sacred religious institution such as marriage because they are gods. They believe they have the right to decide whether Terri Schiavo lives or dies because they are gods. Basically what it boils down to is this: *The essence of liberalism is pride.* Pride is the all-governing element encompassing the religion of liberalism. They hate the idea of having to kowtow to someone else because they feel that they are the authorities of the universe (but not as important as animals of course).

In the forward to his book *Witness,* heroic ex-Communist Whittaker Chambers wrote: "[Communism] is, in fact, man's second oldest faith. Its promise was whispered in the first days of the Creation under the Tree of the Knowledge of Good and Evil: 'Ye shall be as gods.' It is the great alternative faith of mankind. Like all great faiths, its force derives from a simple vision. Other ages have had great visions. They have always been different versions of the same vision: the vision of God and man's relationship to God. The Communist vision is the vision of Man without God."

Aside from pride, other alternative definitions for liberalism are narcissism, vanity (reflect on the fact that 99.8 percent of celebrities are liberals), despotism, debauchery, hedonism and Epicureanism. To explain the last definition, in Ancient Greece there were two categorically dissimilar schools of thought—Epicureanism and Stoicism. The Stoics believed that life should be lived for a greater purpose and that pain should be passively endured, while the Epicureans believed that the greatest good in life was pleasure. It is the same way with liberals, which is why they insist on engaging in hedonistic practices like fornication, adultery, sodomy, drug use, and watching CBS News.

Liberalism is one of the most enigmatic social paradoxes inasmuch as it incorporates both anarchy and fascism. Liberals are anarchists insofar as they believe in no higher authority judging them by their actions, and they are fascists insofar as they are insatiable suckers for control, power and dominion—just like their friends Fidel Castro and "Uncle Joe" Stalin (as Franklin Roosevelt called him). This is manifested by their dogmatic insistence on making law after law after law over the most tedious and preposterous things, such as their outrageous laws against smoking in public (in California, it is illegal to smoke in bars—*bars*) and the most infuriating and unconstitutional rules against carrying concealed weapons in public. They also empower fascist organizations like the ACLU and gush over the United Nations. (You will find more U.N. flags on the front of liberals' houses than you will American flags.)

Liberals are pressing for a new world order. A world governed by the U.N. (even though they don't care if some if its most vital resolutions, such as Resolution 1441, aren't enforced), indoctrinated into the religion of liberalism (or "progressivism" as they call it—we will cover that in the next chapter), inured to the hegemonic standards of "tolerance" and political correctness, where Muslim fanatics are free to run amok because *they are people too,* and where Christian fundamentalism is banned and where Christianity itself is completely mutilated, disfigured and molded into a denomination of the greater religion of liberalism. This may not be our true fate, but—at the risk of sounding like Hal Lindsay—this potential outcome could be vitally integral to the end times.

CHAPTER 2

"PROGRESSIVISM" AND "TOLERANCE" DEFINED

Inasmuch as liberalism denotes the intrinsic human ambition to be "like God" (Genesis 3:5), aside from Islamic terrorists, all angry dictatorial savages are and have been liberals—in their relentless, blood-spattered pursuits of God's throne: Vladimir Lenin, Joseph Stalin, Adolf Hitler, Fidel Castro and Howard Dean, just to name a few. Even the tyrannical religious European monarchs of centuries ago can be considered liberal in that they greatly overestimated the power of man, not taking into account man's inherent fallibility, and smugly presuming that God had given them the divine power to rule over nations. The notion of human supremacy—even if apportioned by a deity—is a very liberal and humanistic construct. But not all liberals are angry dictatorial savages. There are many decent, socially conservative, church-going devout Christians who have been infected with the disease of liberalism. In fact, lately, there has been an uprising of pastors, churches and church-goers who obliviously place community and diversity on a pedestal above preaching the gospels. Churches have barbeques, social functions and outreach programs while rendering solid biblical teaching a subordinate priority. It's all about attracting new visitors and less about giving them what they need when they have them there.

On Easter Sunday, 2004, at a church in my hometown of Oakland, California, the head pastor spent the first fifty minutes of an hour-long sermon telling amusing anecdotes about his vacations and how many hot dogs the youth minister ate at an A's game. Then at the fifty-minute mark, he said, "Oh and I know you're all expecting me to get into the God stuff at this point ..." When he did, one of the things he said was, "The reason Jesus came here was to bring peace." (Apparently Christ was just trying to frighten us with all that "sword" talk.) In fact, on the pamphlets handed out to the attendees, there was an illustration of a dove above the words "Peace is Possible." (I suppose they were originally going to put a picture of Christ on the cross but decided that depicting violence was ungodly.)

Virtually every sermon churches have been preaching for the past few years have been about what God can do for us, not one has been about sin and salvation and what we can do for God. Satan is *never* mentioned, ever. This is a clear-cut example of how liberalism—the religion of the Self—has infected well-meaning and good-intentioned pastors, churches and Christians. "Progressive" Christians are thinking too much about how God can improve their lives instead of how they can better become reflections of God's spirit in the world.

One of the most hauntingly prophetic films I have seen is *A Thief in the Night,* a low-budget Jesus movement film from 1972 about the coming of the rapture and the theoretically subsequent tribulation. One of the characters, Reverend Matthew Turner, is a pastor whose sermons focus on togetherness and love while dismissing the Bible as non-literal and who claims that to take scripture literally is "to box one's self in." One of liberals' ways of not respecting Christianity while pretending to respect Christianity is by claiming that the Bible is "a good work of literature." A few years ago, an atheist English professor of mine made the King James Bible required reading for the class. They like to claim that the stories in the Bible are purely allegorical, but that "much can be learned from them."

Most aggravating is when liberals say Jesus was just "a good teacher." Right. And if Noam Chomsky and Ward Churchill flipped out and claimed that they were the sons of God and that those who worshiped them would have eternal life, would liberals still call them "good teachers"? Well, on second thought, they probably would …

When they're not patronizingly trying to cater to Christians while simultaneously dismissing their faith as hogwash, or for that matter trying to act as if they know anything about Christianity, liberals are bullying Christians into being more "tolerant" and "open-minded." Most embarrassingly, Christians are falling for it. In late 2004, the United Church of Christ (UCC) in San Francisco aired an ad on television in which two bouncers in front of a church are letting in two girls and a heterosexual couple but turning away others, including two men holding hands. A message reads, "Jesus didn't turn people away. Neither do we." The camera then pans over a crowd of diverse UCC members, one of which is a woman who puts her arm around another woman and a voiceover states, "No matter who you are, or where you are on life's journey, you are welcome here." (And no, this was not an ad for hell.)

Liberals promote the notion that the quality of a church should be measured on the basis of how many lesbians, gays, transsexuals, transvestites, zoophiles and other perverts they let into their holy place of worship. I have a better idea: How about we force liberal celebrities to reserve front-row seats for all the homeless punk rockers on Hollywood Boulevard at the next Academy Awards ceremony?

Now if anyone has noticed, avowed atheistic liberals tend to blatantly and obnoxiously take scripture out of context to knock the Gospels. For instance, Chris Hedges writes in his book *American Fascists: The Christian Right and the War on America,* "Hatred of Jews and other non-Christians pervades the Gospel of John (3:18-20). Jews, he wrote, are children of the devil, the father of lies (John 8:39-44)." Apparently Hedges was hoping his readers would take his word and not bother to look up this scripture inasmuch as the two verses he cited specifically involve Christ teaching his disciples that whoever believes in the Father is not condemned and that the true children of God follow his commandments. I don't exactly think that after speaking these words, Christ made a public apology including a request to meet with Jewish leaders to find "the appropriate path for healing." Oh, and unlike Hedges, I am not at all hesitant to encourage my readers to look up those verses to substantiate my interpretation.

On the other hand, however, while avowedly atheistic liberals twist scripture to accommodate their groundless hatred towards Christianity, "progressive" Christians twist scripture to accommodate their convenient, humanistic, politically correct belief system. This is a quintessential trait exhibited by "progressives": Their inherent, inextricable compulsion to take Christ's words out of context and completely disregard other parts of scripture that negate the conclusions they have contrived from the verses that happen to appeal more to them—whether or not they understand what those verses actually mean.

In I Corinthians 5:9-13, the Apostle Paul writes, "I have written you in my letter not to associate with sexually immoral people—not at all meaning the people of this world who are immoral, or the greedy and swindlers, or idolaters. In that case you would have to leave this world. But now I am writing you that you must not associate with anyone who calls himself a brother but is sexually immoral or greedy, an idolater or a slanderer, a drunkard or a swindler. With such a man do not even eat. What business is it of mine to judge those outside the church? Are you not to judge those inside? God will judge those outside. 'Expel the wicked man from among you.'"

Liberals vituperatively accuse conservative Christians of being "judgmental," often citing Matthew 7:1, which reads, "Judge not lest ye be judged." This ties in with liberals' fanatical obsession with the words "discriminate" and "discrimination" (formerly positive terms that are now deemed pejorative). They feel that any form of judgment or discrimination is tantamount to genocide. Well it is certain that Jesus did in fact warn us to leave the judgment of souls up to God, but he never said anything about discrimination. Nor did he condemn judgment within the church, which Paul clearly exonerates. It is a Christian's *duty* to be discriminating. On matters of race? No. On matters of gender? No. On matters of lifestyle? Correctomundo. Liberals assume that the only form of discrimination is racial discrimination, and that the other kind of discrimination—discrimination against gays, is "homophobic."

But to assure them: No one is *afraid* of gays. (Save for the sadomasochists. They're a bit unpleasant.) Gays are the sweetest, gentlest, most harmless creatures on the planet. It's just that the ones who practice being gay don't belong in a church if they claim to be Christians until they're ready to start at least trying to clean up their act.

"Tolerance" has become the central tenet of the religion of liberalism, so much that it's slowly becoming the new world order. In late 1995, the Member States of the United Nations Educational, Scientific and Cultural Organization met in Paris at the twenty-eighth session of the General Conference to discuss the importance of "tolerance." Their definition of "tolerance" was "respect, acceptance and appreciation of the rich diversity of our world's cultures" and that it "is not only a moral duty, it is also a political and legal requirement." (Not that they were fascists or anything.) They also stated that "Tolerance involves the rejection of dogmatism and *absolutism*" (emphasis mine). So basically, the definition of tolerance is only tolerating those who subscribe to relativism while being intolerant of absolutists (i.e. Christians) on the basis that they are intolerant and "pose a global threat." (And some are actually suggesting that we withdraw from the U.N.! *Pchh …)*

Also documenting the global threat of absolutist Christian intolerance is Dr. Teresa Whitehurst, who wrote in a January 25, 2005 column titled "The Intolerance of Christian Conservatives," "Conservative Christianity has morphed into Old Testament rigidity and eternally enforced morality, not guided nor even tempered by the interpersonal acceptance, tolerance of social outcasts, and deeper spiritual understanding that Jesus taught and modeled."

Pastor Dan Secrist has a different angle. Secrist, who has been the senior pastor at Faith Assembly of Lacey, Washington for over thirty-five years, participated as a chaplain in the Washington State Legislature. State officials began whining about the prayers he delivered at the legislature, yet legislators who walked out while a Muslim delivered a prayer were criticized by the public. As Secrist later stated, "Jesus put an exclusive claim on truth. And if tolerance becomes the new truth, then there is no such thing as truth. Each person makes up his own moral code, and everyone else is supposed to be okay with it. Nobody's opinion can be superior to another. Nobody can be incorrect. But Jesus was very exclusive when he said, 'I am the way, the truth and the life. No man comes to the Father but by me' (John 14:6). He said there was such a thing as absolute truth. He said he personified that truth. He claimed to be the only expert."

It seems to be the concept of absolutism that liberals are so whiny about. No wonder they have perpetuated the senatorial career of Ted Kennedy for so long, to whom the term "absolute" is a brand name for vodka. Liberals have no concept of discernment—between good and evil, right and wrong, black and white, Bill Clinton and Jesus Christ, et cetera. They go through life never drawing any conclusions—except that Republicans are fascists, Donald Rumsfeld should be fired, and Barbra Streisand is a good singer.

Baptist minister Tony Campolo, spiritual counselor to Bill Clinton (his last job was being an orthopedist for Stevie Wonder), said in a July 2004 interview that "Christians need to be considering other issues beside abortion and homosexuality." He continued by saying that "the overwhelming proportion of the gay community that love Jesus, that go to church, that are deeply committed in spiritual things, try to change and can't change." (Which is basically like telling a kid with cerebral palsy that he should give up because he can never get laid.) He went on by saying, "the Church acts as though they are just stubborn and unwilling, when in reality they can't change. To propose that every gay with proper counseling and proper prayer can change their orientation is to create a mentality where parents are angry with their children, saying, 'You are a gay person because you don't want to change and you're hurting your mother and your father and your family and you're embarrassing us all.'" "These young people cannot change. What they are begging for, and what we as Church people have a responsibility to give them, is loving affirmation as they are."

Another church infected with the malignant cancers of liberalism is the Park Slope United Methodist Church (UMC) in Brooklyn, which announced in September, 2001 that the church would no longer conduct legal marriages in its sanctuary nor would its pastor, the Rev. Elizabeth Braddon, perform marriages or holy union ceremonies at all. This was in protest of the United Methodist policy that prohibits homosexual unions in UMC sanctuaries and bars the denomination's clergy from conducting such unions.

The church stated that it "will work to remove discriminatory policies in the UMC Book of Discipline," and that marriages and same-sex unions would be held in "places other than in our church, such as churches of other denominations, private homes, the garden, or parks and other public spaces." This church described itself as "a community of faith of about 200 members from diverse backgrounds exploring together many ways of understanding God ... celebrating the gifts of all persons regardless of sexual orientation or gender identity.... We honor a diversity of theological expression, and use both feminine and masculine images of God." The church also boasts that it "has created rituals in the worship that reflect the spiritual diversity of our members," including Native American chanting, drumming and a Caribbean Harvest festival. Oh, and all that Jesus stuff.

And more recently, in June 2006, when asked if homosexuality was a sin, another "Christian" leader who clearly doesn't believe reading the Bible is essential to being a Christian, Katharine Jefferts Schori, bishop of the Diocese of Nevada, the first woman leader of the 2.3 million-member Episcopal Church, replied, "I don't believe so. I believe that God creates us with different gifts. Each one of us comes into this world with a different collection of things that challenge us and things that give us joy and allow us to bless the world around us." When asked about passages in the Bible which deemed homosexuality sinful, she said, "The Bible has a great deal to teach us about how to live as human beings. The Bible does not have so much to teach us about what sorts of food to eat, what sorts of clothes to wear—there are rules in the Bible about those that we don't observe today ... The Bible tells us about how to treat other human beings, and that's certainly the great message of Jesus—to include the unincluded." Seeing as the "unincluded" also includes pedophiles and rapists, does that mean we should "include" them too? Oh, that's right, the Catholic Church already has dibs on them.

Not only have liberals assaulted Christianity through ACLU lawsuits, as has been documented in David Limbaugh's book as well as my documentary, but they have bitched and whined about Christianity being confiscated from them like a baby having its milk bottle taken away (even though the baby is lactose intolerant). They are attempting to infiltrate Christianity and nullify it to the degree, as I said earlier, of being just another subsidiary denomination of the religion of liberalism. Perhaps it's a sneaky way of taking back the evangelical vote—by forcing the evangelicals to become like them. Well it is about time for them to be called on it before Billy Graham becomes a Clinton-loving Democrat.

CHAPTER 3

"COMFORTABLE CHRISTIANITY"

Christians are often too afraid to talk to non-believers about sin and salvation, because liberals don't feel like they need to be saved from anything. They are Judd Nelson in *The Breakfast Club,* not caring how many more Saturdays he will have to spend at school for disobeying Principal Vernon. They are gods, remember? Situationalists. Morality to them is relative. In his 1651 book *Leviathan,* the English philosopher Thomas Hobbes wrote, "For the laws of nature (as justice, equity, modesty, mercy, and, in sum, doing to others as we would be done to) of themselves, without the terror of some power, to cause them to be observed, are contrary to our natural passions; that carry us to partiality, pride, revenge and the like."

To the contrary, liberals subscribe to the Rousseauian notion that man is inherently good and is in no need of salvation. (It is no coincidence that Rousseau was one of the inspirations for the French Revolution—a cultural eruption that resulted in the imprisonments and massacres of priests throughout France.)

So "progressive" Christians choose to not talk about sin and salvation. They instead talk about other more comfortable virtues of Christianity, such as love, sharing, and forgiveness. (Liberals may know nothing about these things either, but at least they sound nice.) Satan is completely non-existent to liberals (even though many of them practically worship him), validating what Kevin Spacey said in *The Usual Suspects*: "The greatest trick the devil ever played was convincing the world that he didn't exist." In addition, whenever anyone refers to the name "Satan," "the devil," or any terminology from the Book of Revelation they are instantaneously derided as fundamentalist Neanderthals.

One hilarious and dead-on satirization (not a word but I'm using it anyway) of this new, popular brand of "comfortable Christianity" was in Kevin Smith's film *Dogma,* in which a Catholic priest—played by George Carlin—presents to his congregation the "Buddy Christ," which is a statue of Christ giving a wink, a smile and a thumbs-up. The priest explains that the whole crucifixion thing was just so dark and depressing and that the church needed to replace it with something more uplifting.

Even many Christians are practically convinced that Satan doesn't exist, or at least they act like they are. Seldom is he mentioned in many churches, seldom is he mentioned in many youth groups. It seems that the only occasions upon which we hear anything about Satan is when we listen to Southern Baptist ministers, and people in the South already have it all together anyway. Not to mention—recent polls indicate that very few Americans can even locate hell on a map! (Their usual guess is Oxnard, California.)

There are deeper reasons for why liberals get so uncomfortable about Christianity. Ephesians 5:8 reads, "For you were once darkness, but now you are light in the Lord. Live as children of light (for the fruit of the light consists in all goodness, righteousness and truth)." I was once a child of the darkness, and while my political views were to the right, I was engulfed in a liberalistic mindset that kept me in the darkness. Big time. My lifestyle could have cost me my life, and it literally *did* cost a close friend his life whom I had set a poor example for, and the things I did in that part of my life left me with some major regrets that can never be taken care of. So I know what it is to feel the shame that brings on the darkness, for it is, indeed, shame that brings on darkness. That is why seedy bars, strip clubs, and hedonistic parties are always dimmed and dark. Liberals are like Adam and Eve when they became aware of their nakedness. There are four essential factors for as to why liberals are uncomfortable with Christianity: 1) Shame, 2) Humiliation, 3) Denial, and of course, 4) Pride. That is why they dwell in darkness—and that is why they will be *really* ashamed, humiliated, cognizant and humbled when they are brought into the light and exposed at the time of Christ's coming. As for now, they are like ditzy blonde cheerleaders in life. While we as Christians are called to serve a greater purpose in life, liberals just want to have some fun until the sun comes up over Santa Monica Boulevard.

As we discussed in the last chapter, "progressive" Christians don't like to *judge,* which is appropriate of them outside the church. But even more so, they pusillanimously shy away from discriminating against anyone who lives a deviant lifestyle, no matter how deviant that lifestyle is. They seem to assume that judging and discriminating are the same thing. To discriminate is to be observant of someone's words and deeds and to determine for one's self whether or not such behavior should be emulated. To judge is to decide whether that person should go to hell or not, which is obviously up to the Lord. But discrimination is not necessarily a bad thing—it should really be a positive term. Just because you make the observation that Frankie and Chester are engaging in behavior that wouldn't be appropriate for network television doesn't mean you're judging the fate of their souls, and doesn't mean you don't still love them. (Actually, I take back the network television analogy.) But at the same time, just because you love them doesn't mean they're not going to burn in hell. Starting to make sense?

Christians need to be willing to discriminate if they want to take notes on how they should and shouldn't present themselves to the world. They need to be willing to fight to defend their religion against the imminent wave of "progressivism" that is whitewashing their religion. They also need to be willing to fight to protect nonbelievers from scriptural distortions made by the ACLU, Americans United for Separation of Church and State, People for the American Way, and Michael Newdow. Christ did not call us to be wimps. That's Congressman Jack Murtha's job. Being a wimp is not what the "turn the other cheek" verse encourages. Instead, one is to be "a good soldier in Christ" (II Timothy 2:3).

One of the classic examples of Christians caving in to liberal harassment and nullifying their representations of Christ is when Mel Gibson released a re-cut version of *The Passion of the Christ* in March 2005, eliminating five minutes of footage that was hard to stomach for many people. This was apparently in acquiescence to snobby liberal critics who complained that the film was "extremely sadistic" (David Denby, *New Yorker*), "sadomasochistic" (Jonathan Foreman, *New York Post*), a "wasted exercise in sadomasochism" (Al Neuharth, *USA Today*), an exercise in "high-minded sadomasochism" (A.O. Scott, *New York Times*) and "sadism" (David Ansen, *Newsweek*) and a "repulsive masochistic fantasy" and "sacred snuff film" (Leon Wieseltier, *New Republic*), which "would horrify the regulars at an S&M club." Liberals seem to have sadomasochism on their minds quite a bit. Perhaps the quote really goes: "*If you're a conservative before eighteen you have no heart, if you're a liberal past thirty you're a bitter freak who has delusions of sexual bestiality on a frequent basis.*"

To censor the exhibition of the pain Christ endured for us even by five minutes is a gesture of selfishness and ingratitude. Jesus said, "Take up your cross and follow me!" (Matthew 16:24) How are we to take up our crosses if we don't have the willingness to experience watching a portrayal of Christ taking up his? Liberals don't care what Christ went through to give us eternal life; they would rather be watching *Brokeback Mountain* and lamenting over those poor adulterous gay cowboys whose practices our society was intolerant enough to frown upon. Basically, Gibson responded to the raging liberals the way the Spanish responded to the raging Muslim lunatics after the Madrid attacks—with classic Chamberlain-esque appeasement.

"Progressive" Christians make the mistake of trying to make a religion comfortable that is simply not supposed to be comfortable. Sure, Christ's abiding love is comforting, and the knowledge of him is the most comfortable feeling one could ever experience, but that doesn't make Christianity a comfortable religion. Why is it that liberals stare at the floor every time Christianity is brought up? *Christianity was not meant to be a comfortable religion.* Christianity professes that humans are worthless without God. That they are inherently corrupt. That they are subject to eternal damnation if they don't know who their daddy is. And God has not always been a comforter. In the book of Joshua he ordered preemptive wars, wiping out innocent civilians—many of them women and children. In Leviticus he ordered the sacrificing of lambs. (Oh dear! Call PETA!) Even Jesus himself, in a fit of rage, turned over tables, yelled and whipped people. God is very merciful, but he can also be a badass.

We even have sanctimonious snobs like Chris Hedges attempting to bully Christian leaders into rendering vital portions of scripture obsolete. In *American Fascists,* he writes, "Church leaders must denounce the biblical passages that champion apocalyptic violence and hateful political creeds. They must do so in the light of other biblical passages that teach a compassion and tolerance, often exemplified in the life of Christ, which stands opposed to bigotry and violence. Until this happens, until the Christian churches wade into the debate, these biblical passages will be used by bigots and despots to give sacred authority to their calls to subjugate or eradicate the enemies of God. This literature in the biblical canon keeps alive the virus of hatred, whether dormant or active, and the possibility of apocalyptic terror in the name of God. And the steady refusal by churches to challenge the canonical authority of these passages means these churches share some of the blame." Charles Manson loved "Helter Skelter." Does this mean those long-haired liberal darlings "share some of the blame" for the Tate-LaBianca murders?

"Progressive" Christians simply need to stop trying to water down Christianity to make it more comfortable. Less money funds should be apportioned to repainting the church from brown to green (green is just so much more *inviting!*), less money needs to be spent tearing down and rebuilding the sanctuary to make it more "modern." Aging elders of the church need to stop being forced into silence because their ideas are "outdated." Christians need to simply live lives pleasing to the Lord and be ready to defend his commandments without beating around the bush or claiming that they are not entirely literal. This is carrying the cross of Christ—unhesitantly and unapologetically.

CHAPTER 4

LIBERALISM: THE RELIGION OF FEELINGS

It is a wonder how swiftly and surely so many Christians are swept off their feet and dropped into the trenches of disbelief, half-assed Christianity and Mormonism. There is a way, it seems, that those Bible-pushing used car salesmen successfully drag innocent victims into their freaky-deaky Latter-Day Saints trips and getting them to buy into crackpot fantasies some crazy Northeastern white guy had eighteen centuries after Christ died and left us with everything we should need. One of the things they guarantee is a "visit from the Holy Ghost" should the victim pray about the possible truth of what is written in the Book of Mormon. There must be a way that the devil works through that cult inasmuch as Christian converts to Mormonism tend to claim that they *feel* the presence of God much more than they did when they were Christians.

In religion, there has been a profound contemporary emphasis on *feelings*. This is a result of the impact liberalism has had on religion throughout this generation. Liberals, as Epicureans, predicate the basis of their very existence on feelings. This is why liberals, elevating political correctness to the highest pedestal, insist on saying *"Neecawrawgwaw"*—they don't want to hurt anyone's *feelings*. More pertinently, it is also why they shamelessly gobble up drugs, promote "safe sex" (a euphemism for gay or underage sex), and have sexual relations with "that woman." The notion of a higher power (as he is conveniently called in Alcoholics Anonymous) just gets in their way of getting plastered Saturday night and waking up Sunday morning next to a broad named "Trixie" while forty percent of Americans are in church.

While Christians say, "Forgive us our trespasses," liberals say, "If it feels good, do it!" While liberalism is the religion of pride, godlessness and the self, it is also the religion of feelings. That is why when liberals march into church, they expect the kind of euphoric experience they get from chewing peyote buttons while listening to Pink Floyd. And their obsession with feelings has spattered the faith of their religious pawns—the "progressive" Christians, whose patience in a church service is contingent upon how much the Holy Spirit intoxicates their minds.

As I said earlier, liberalism is the religion of the Self. This is why "progressive" Christians are more concerned with what they can get out of being a Christian than what God can get out of their being followers of him. This is why so many weak-minded Christians lose their faith when the epiphanic sensations of embracing the Holy Spirit subside.

Indeed, what is almost as difficult, and in some cases more difficult, than becoming a Christian, is *remaining* a Christian. When someone becomes a Christian, they are commonly blessed with an epiphanic sensation of spiritual euphoria that further solidifies their faith. But with time, this sensation proves to be transitory. Inasmuch as many born-again Christians make the mistake of obliviously allowing the strength of their faith to become dependent upon that sensation, when the sensation evaporates, their faith recedes with it. As a result, they become lethargic in their faith, and return to the materialistic mindset that preceded their conversion or rebirth. What is even worse, returning to God is then more difficult than ever.

What "progressive" Christians don't understand is that the frequency of the manifestation of the Holy Spirit is not in their control, nor should it be. God will decide when he wants to make himself blatantly obvious to us as he probably did during our respective rebirths. Christians must submit to God and wait patiently for the fruits of their abiding faith to materialize. The verse they must arm themselves with is Hebrews 3:14, which says: "We have come to share in Christ if we hold firmly till the end the confidence we had at first."

In Matthew 13:4-8, Jesus tells the parable of the farmer who went out to sow his seed. "As he was scattering the seed, some fell along the path, and the birds came and ate it up. Some fell on rocky places, where it did not have much soil. It sprang up quickly, because the soil was shallow. But when the sun came up, the plants were scorched, and they withered because they had no root. Other seed fell among thorns, which grew up and choked the plants. Still other seed fell on good soil, where it produced a crop—a hundred, sixty or thirty times what was sown." Christians should endeavor to be like the seed that fell on good soil, and keep on keeping on throughout spiritual empty stomachs.

In an October 1996 volume of *Issues, Etc. Journal,* Don Matzat wrote an article called "Feelings, Emotions and Christian Truth" in which he said: "There is nothing wrong with Christians desiring feelings, emotions, and experience. In fact, the lack of any experience is in itself an experience. The lack of feeling is a feeling. The lack of emotion is an emotion. Any cursory reading of the New Testament demonstrates that love, joy, peace, hope, contentment are to be the Christian's experience, feeling, and emotion.

"Yet, that same reading of the New Testament will also demonstrate that feelings and emotions are an *effect* and not a *cause*. All of the imperatives or commands of Scripture are based upon the indicatives, or the doctrinal statements of what God has done for us. In other words, the subjective feelings and emotions commanded in the Word of God *must be* the result of embracing in faith the objective doctrinal facts of what God has done in Christ Jesus. Feelings and emotions that arise because of a group dynamic involving lively music and expressive demonstrations are no different than the feelings and emotions that arise at a rock concert. They are not the fruit of the Spirit."

Matzat goes on to quote Martin Luther, who writes, "We must not judge by what we feel or by what we see before us. The Word must be followed, and we must firmly hold that these truths are to be believed, not experienced; for to believe is not to experience. Not indeed that what we believe is never to be experienced but that faith is to precede experience. And the Word must be believed even when we feel and experience what differs entirely from the Word." Luther further writes, "Feeling must follow, but faith, apart from feeling, must be there first."

Liberals preside over a religion of feelings and their "progressive" pawns are attempting to transform Christianity into a religion of feelings too—a religion in which we do not put on the armor of Christ unless the armor fits comfortably; in which we do not want to die to sin unless it's of old age. It is only a matter of time before "progressive" Christians go into spiritual withdrawal and decide the whole Jesus thing just isn't "doing it" for them anymore. As Bob Dylan wrote in one of his ballsier songs during his late '70s/early '80s born-again trip, "He's the property of Jesus—Resent him to the bone—You got something better—You've got a heart of stone."

CHAPTER 5

THE MYTH OF THE "OPEN MIND"

The slogan of the United Methodist Church is: "Open hearts. Open minds. Open doors." (Now let's all repeat those six words together followed by a collective flowery orgasmic sigh of euphoric tranquility. *Huuuuuhhh!*) One of the unwritten prerequisites to becoming a liberal is adopting what has become the golden calf of liberalism: the "open mind." Of course, like all tenets of liberalism, this one comes with a double standard. Liberals pride themselves on having "open minds" when it comes to science (or better put: evolution and Darwinism), religion (or better put: Islam, paganism and "progressive" Christianity), culture (or better put: anything that's as far from Anglo-Saxon Protestant culture as possible), lifestyles (or better put: alternative lifestyles that involve male-on-male sodomy and lesbian fisting), and art (or better put: crucifixes submerged in urine and paintings of the Virgin Mary surrounded by pornographic images and elephant sh—).

According to liberal theology, an open mind may be "open," but it has high-voltage motion censors that sense any intrusion of creationism, conservatism, biblical Christianity, political incorrectness, discrimination, prudence or purity. Also, if you are convicted of not having an "open mind," you will be slandered, smeared, stigmatized and censured. But don't fret! There are multiple formulas for developing this requisite, sacrosanct "open mind." In an online how-to manual, a website called Wikihow.com prescribes Scrabble, juggling, playing with magnets, left-handed ping-pong, and dumpster diving.

We also have strong, devoted teachers in our education system who are doing their part to harvest a rising generation of "open minds" that will create a better, safer, healthier future for our nation. An organization which promotes "gay, lesbian, bisexual and transgender" practices for children and teens held a conference a few years ago, at which one speaker, Wayne Palowski, director of training for the *Schutzstaffel*—I mean—Planned Parenthood of America (sorry, slip of the

17

fingers), declared that "boys should be encouraged to use condoms and mastur-bate at home so they will develop skills for future sex acts." All this before express-ing support for the idea of schools teaching these boys such skills during sex-ed classes. If only Mark Foley wasn't a Republican, liberals would be desperately recruiting him to teach at their little nurseries-for-pedophiles that are otherwise described as "public schools." Come to think of it, I don't think it's just open *minds* liberal schoolteachers are wanting from their students ...

Also, many are working to keep the workplace open exclusively to those with "open minds." The Minnesota Department of Corrections has made it a require-ment for its employees to attend training sessions called "Gays and Lesbians in the Workplace," which are mandatory edifications put in place to ensure that cer-tain designated standards of tolerance and acceptance are met in the workplace. Isn't it just so reassuring to know that the only people who can get fired from the workplace now are the ones whose minds aren't "open" enough to just look the other way when one of their fellow employees of the same sex makes repeated threats to report them to the employers for sexual orientation discrimination if they continually refuse to join them at the Over the Rainbow Club at 9 p.m. in St. Paul?

When I was in high school, my administrators practically made us heterosexu-als feel like we were missing out on something. And sometimes I really did feel like I was missing out, given the social protection, lifestyle glorification and female attention all the gay guys got. Hell, assemblies were held in honor of gays—not only that, but the gays got a "Day of Silence." If I could get everyone to shut the hell up for a whole day just for me, I wouldn't have to spend all this time writing a book to get my thoughts out.

Liberals love to brag about how "open" their "minds" are. Well I completely understand. They have got to let some air in, otherwise those minds of theirs would be too suffocating and claustrophobic for the poor little lonely dust parti-cles that reside in them. It's interesting how an agnostic friend of mine, whom I screen films for all the time, who prides himself on his "open mind" and believes that everyone should be "open-minded," is interestedly waiting for me to me show him *The Last Temptation of Christ* but for some reason is in no hurry for me to show him *The Passion of the Christ*. Having an "open mind," after all, is about embracing all that which is contrary to what is preached in the Gospels but leav-ing no capacity for the truth written in the Gospels. Perhaps they feel that such truth would irrevocably *close* their minds and act as a barricade against the income of more important information such as masturbation skills and the art of dumpster diving.

A mind is an analog camera. If you open it up, you expose the film and it gets ruined. The film is the human soul. The more it's exposed to the fruitless deeds of darkness and the evil that governs the world, the more it will be corrupted. In Matthew 22:37, Jesus says, "'Love the Lord your God with all your heart and with all your soul and with all your mind.'" If we open our hearts, our souls and our minds to that which negates that love for God, then our hearts, souls and minds will be corrupted and the Spirit which replenishes these three vital instruments will depart. On a consistent basis, Christians are following the trend of "progressivism" and finding shame in their religion as liberals attach stigmas of racism, homophobia and oppression to it, and in due course are feeling pressured into worshiping and promoting the golden calf of liberalism called the "open mind" at the expense of their relationship with Christ. Perhaps out of it they get better at playing ping-pong with their left hands and the young get better at doing something else with their hands but it certainly doesn't sound like a fair trade to me.

CHAPTER 6

CHISTIANITY (D)

Since religion isn't exactly their strong suit, liberals attack it. And when they get caught attacking it, they pretend that they actually *are* religious.

Now you don't have to be conservative in the traditional sense to be a Christian. This is to say, you don't have to support supply-side economics, capital punishment or the war in Iraq to be a true follower. In fact, you can even support "a woman's right to choose" (although if you do you're seriously confused).

However, when you become a Christian, even if you are a liberal Democrat, you have to some degree inexorably adopted a conservative mentality inasmuch as although you may still embrace certain tenets of liberalism or think John Edwards is hot, you have outright rejected the very core of liberalism, which is pride in man and repudiation of God; essentially, you have embraced the notion that man is not at the center of the universe. Not to mention, your consideration of the ACLU as an actual "civil liberties" group will slowly but surely deteriorate. (Quite possibly, you may begin to see it more as a Satanic cult of blood-drinking death-worshipers and wonder how one of the presidents you voted for could think to put one of them on the Supreme Court—but that's further down the road.)

But this does not excuse the many Democratic politicians such as Howard Dean, Bill Clinton, Al Gore, Jimmy Carter, Hillary Clinton and others from either masquerading as Christians, setting dreadful examples as Christians, or interpreting the Bible in the same way a seven-year-old would interpret one of Michio Kaku's books on the study of theoretical physics.

An example of the latter is when during the 2000 presidential campaign, in defense of his quixotic views on the environment, Al Gore said, "In my faith tradition, it is written in the book of Matthew, 'Where your heart is, there's your treasure also.' And I believe that we ought to recognize the value to our children and grandchildren of taking steps that preserve the environment in a way that's good for them." Not to mention teaching our children and grandchildren that their "treasure" should be in the world (hence the "environment") and not in heaven.

And Jesus is really regretting not visiting the earth during this generation so Howard Dean could have been one of his disciples. During the 2004 election, Dean (whose favorite book of the New Testament is "the Book of Job") came closer than any of the other candidates to literally exonerating homosexuality—openly that is. While the case with the other candidates was that they were "against gay marriage" but would have no problem conducting a gay wedding ceremony or for that matter being the videographer for the couple's private post-reception wedding night festivities, in January 2004, Dean said, "From a religious point of view … if God had thought homosexuality is a sin, he would not have created gay people." Well by that rationale, if God had thought anger and rage were sins, he wouldn't have created raging, firebreathing psychopaths either. Guess you're off the hook, Dean!

Ready to fumingly head-butt through the wall anyone who questioned him on the basis of his aforementioned talking points, in an interview with Tim Russert on *Meet the Press* in May 2005, Dean insisted, "I don't go to church all that much. I consider myself a deeply religious person. I consider myself a Christian. And I don't—you know, some of the other Christians would dare to say that I'm not a Christian. Frankly, it's what gets my ire up. We get back to the Rush Limbaugh stuff. I am sick of being told what I am and what I'm not by other people. I'll tell you what I am. I'm a committed Christian. And the fact of whether I go to church or not, people can say whether I should or shouldn't, I worship in my own way. It came out in the campaign that I pray every night. That's my business. That's not the business of the Pharisees who are going to preach to me about what I do and then do something else."

While he's not snobbishly calling the GOP "pretty much a white, Christian party," Dean is going on Pat Robertson's show, *The 700 Club,* claiming that Democrats "have an enormous amount in common with the Christian community, and particularly with the evangelical Christian community." Well sure, if you don't count the fact that the Democratic Party supports fetal massacres in abortion clinics, "gay marriage," the "separation of church and state" and opposes school vouchers and the death penalty, those Christians and those Dems sure seem like soul mates!

"I think what we have in common with the evangelical community is that we ought to have a lot fewer abortions than we do," Dean continued. Sure, instead of an average of one million abortions per year, let's cut it down to 700,000. We're running out of those damn suction catheters!

Dean followed up by saying, "The difference is that we don't think making criminals out of doctors and women is a good idea." And I guess he would think that making "criminals" out of Nazi storm troopers during World War II just wouldn't have been a "good idea" either. Frowning upon their activities would have done just fine.

Similar things were said by impeached former president Bill Clinton, a self-described Christian whom Billy Graham thinks should be an evangelist, when in an ABC interview in March 1994, he said, "I think there are too many abortions in America. I think there should be much more adoption in America. But I do not believe that it is self evident from the Bible that all abortions are murder." Yeah, maybe not *all* of them. Just some of them. After all, perhaps if it weren't for *Roe v. Wade,* fewer babies would have been slaughtered between the seventies and the nineties and there would have been more people in America and hence the possibility of Clinton getting a majority to vote for him in at least one of his elections.

And I'm sure Jesus was just ecstatic about Rev. Clinton's support of the Freedom of Choice Act, which guaranteed abortion rights to women regardless of the Supreme Court's possible reconsideration of *Roe,* overriding existing state regulations and provisions and taking abortion out of the hands of the Supreme Court and the state legislatures that have traditionally regulated it. If that's not a sign of desperation for as many abortions to be conducted as possible without any interruptions, I don't know what is.

Perhaps they truly are curious about Christianity. But it would have to be "curious" as in the way every young boy is "curious" about his friend Bobby at some point. It is truly a shame that the only Democrat their party has produced in the last generation who embodies the character of a true Christian is Zell Miller, and he's barely a Democrat anymore. Democrats' version of Christianity is like WCW wrestling—it doesn't look real and it isn't real either.

CHAPTER 7

HOW LIBERALS TRY TO BULLY CHRISTIANS OUT OF POLITICS

It was always such a rigid custom for adults to say to children over the dinner table, "Don't speak unless spoken to," which is essentially what liberals have been saying to Christians lately (except for the "unless spoken to" part). Liberals have promoted the notion that Christians should only be allowed in government if what they do and what they say is in no way influenced by their faith. This is basically like saying to liberals that they're only allowed in government if what they do isn't influenced by Joseph Stalin and what they say isn't influenced by the guy who said "I am the walrus."

During the 2000 election, George W. Bush made the mistake of giving away his secret plans to institute a totalitarian theocracy where non-believers are stoned (although many of them probably really are stoned at this moment), when he dared to say that his favorite philosopher was Jesus.

Liberals went into such a panic that they looked like they were all going into labor. Apparently caught up in a psycho-analytical frenzy over the outrageous thing Bush had said, on his show, *Hardball,* biblical scholar Chris Matthews cited Matthew 22:21, "Render unto Caesar the things that are Caesar's and to God the things that are Gods." (Matthews has an apparent fixation on that verse inasmuch as he used it on multiple other occasions, including in an interview with Judge Roy Moore in March 2005 and one with Margaret Carlson and Tony Blankley in August 2005.) Apparently Bush gave to the government something that belonged to God by saying Jesus was his favorite philosopher.

After 9/11, a former White House official said in an interview that Bush had said that "God put me here" to fight a war on terrorism. To this, liberals reacted by going into uncontrolled spasms and choking on their own vomit. What kind of sanctimonious clown would think that God has a purpose for him?

Liberals see no purpose in life except to have fun and destroy traditional institutions. (Although the good liberals, or "Barbra Streisand liberals" as I call them, find purpose in charity and serving the poor and needy.) But they can't fathom (or refuse to fathom) the concept of having a purpose that transcends the confines of the material world, and anyone who makes the mistake of sharing their speculations as to God's purpose for them is derided as thinking they're the messiah (which conflicts with liberals' assertion that Bill Clinton is actually the messiah).

When asked if he sought advice from his father in fighting the second war on Iraq, Bush replied, "There is a higher father that I appeal to." In a BBC film, a former Palestinian foreign minister, Nabil Shaath, said that Bush told a Palestinian delegation in 2003 that God spoke to him and said, "George, go and fight these terrorists in Afghanistan" and also "George, go and end the tyranny in Iraq." (The White House denies that Bush said that.) Whether or not he did say that, liberals snobbishly believed that the war in Iraq was the product of superstitions warping the president's mind.

Apparently liberals aren't aware that God orchestrates and has orchestrated countless wars by speaking to world leaders, as we have read in Exodus, Joshua, Judges, Samuel, and many other books of the Old Testament. And last I checked, there were no annoying McGovernite Israelites with "No Blood for Milk and Honey" bumper stickers on the backs of their caravans calling Moses a "warmonger," screaming "Where are Pharaoh's WMDs?" and claiming that his plan for war against the Egyptians was the product of some "Jewish conspiracy." (And Moses actually was a Jew!) *"Hey, Moses! How was your day? How many kids did you kill today?"*

Whenever someone claims that they feel they are led by God to do something, liberals automatically think that that person is actually claiming that they *are* God, or that God shows favor to them. Liberals also feel that if a Christian in office allows their faith to influence their decisions, they are imposing their values on the nation. On President Bush's second Inauguration Day, BBC News asked a panel of voters to share their views and predictions regarding the Bush administration. Responding to one of the voters, one person from Washington D.C. wrote: "This country was also founded on slavery. Does that mean we should make slavery mandatory for Americans? The problem with Christianity in America is that fundamentalists, like Bush, are trying to force everybody to live according to their religious beliefs, not unlike the Taliban. The Founding Fathers would not approve of the current religious fanaticism." So one minute he's denigrating our country on the basis that its earliest leaders sanctioned slavery while the next minute he's complaining that Bush doesn't live up to the standards of those very leaders. You can tell this person voted for Kerry and it's not just because of his dissatisfaction with Bush. (And by the way, the Mexican government sanctions bull-fighting. Does that mean Mexico was "founded" on bull-fighting?)

I don't know. I personally have a hard time believing that non-Christians are being forced into Christianity by a president who said, "According to Muslim teachings, God first revealed His word in the Holy Qur'an to the prophet, Muhammad, during the month of Ramadan. That word has guided billions of believers across the centuries, and those believers built a culture of learning and literature and science. All the world continues to benefit from this faith and its achievements." Bush declined to name all the achievements because we all know that would take a *long* time …

Liberals would think that if a Christian family invites an atheist over for dinner and the family says their nightly prayer before eating, it's as if that family is tackling the guest, strapping him to a chair and forcing him to listen to an all-night reading of every genealogy in the Old Testament. Liberals are like cats when you mention your faith around them—you make the slightest move (i.e. tapping your toe once, scratching your back, coughing) and the cat jumps on its feet, whips back its ears, puffs its tail and bulges its eyes, ready for attack. They feel they are always at risk of being imposed upon and indoctrinated into some phony cultist belief. (Gee, they must be pretty weak-minded people if they're so easy to indoctrinate. We could have a lot of fun with them!)

Tom Cruise can exclaim publicly that scientology is "the shit, man!" but if a Christian says anything positive about Christianity in front of a liberal, he's automatically discriminating against Islam, Buddhism, Hinduism, atheism and agnosticism all in one breath. Not to mention, he has violated the sacred "separation of church and state." Speaking of which, I might take this time to mention that liberals don't actually read what's in the Constitution. They predicate all their legal and political conclusions on those bottomless penumbras scattered about the document. That's where they've dug up this policy of "separation of church and state" (along with their brilliant vindications of sucking babies' brains out of their skulls).

In 1802, when Thomas Jefferson wrote his letter to the Danbury Baptists, little did he know that he was actually writing a significant part of the Constitution, at least to liberals. Now his famous words "separation of church and state" (with which he was originally implying the protection of the church from the state) are used to impose godlessness upon a country whose Constitution was written, according to second president John Adams, "only for a moral and religious people."

The "separation of church and state" phrases, along with the Establishment Clause of the First Amendment, are both now used as litmus tests for politicians—especially Supreme Court nominees. Around the time Bush nominated John Roberts to the Supreme Court, Americans United for Separation of Church and State (AUSCS) said on its website: "Roberts has consistently advocated abandonment of the 'Lemon test,' which the Supreme Court has applied in Establishment Clause cases for more than thirty years."

It's about time for politicians to think about rendering obsolete the "lemon test," a product of the 1971 *Lemon v. Kurtzman* case, which forbids government officials from acting with a religious agenda, endorsing religion, or excessively entangling government and religion. Americans United continued: "Roberts' elevation to the Court would thus result in *Lemon* being overturned, thereby throwing Establishment Clause jurisprudence into disarray and allowing government officials to endorse, advocate, and engage in religion and religious practices provided that they do not force the active participation of listeners."

Their mention of the Establishment Clause is significant as it relates to AUSCS's fear of "government officials" being allowed to "endorse, advocate [and] engage in religion." Last I checked, all the Establishment Clause said was that "*Congress* shall make no *law* respecting an establishment of religion" (emphases mine). That doesn't prohibit *Supreme Court* justices from "advocating" religion, which could mean anything from allowing Ten Commandments monuments in front of courthouses in Kentucky and Texas to allowing schoolchildren to pass out candy canes to their fellow classmates during Christmas time.

Americans United also gasped that "[w]hile at the Solicitor General's office, Roberts authored a brief arguing that school officials and local clergy should be allowed to deliver prayers at public-school graduation ceremonies." And last I checked, school officials are not *Congress* and prayers are not *laws*.

Liberals have absolutely no reason to fear Christians being in government. There is no record of Christians actually violating the Establishment Clause nor will there ever be probably. The only possible reason as to why liberals are so fearful of Christians being in government is because they despise everything Christians stand for. And that's that.

CHAPTER 8

THE STIGMA OF FUNDAMENTALISM

While conservatives have apparently turned the term "liberal" into a swear word, as many l————s contend, liberals have turned the term "fundamentalist" into a swear word. One of liberals' ways of attacking Christians while pretending not to attack Christians is by using the term "fundamentalist." "Oh, we have nothing against Christians, it's just those *fundamentalists* we want to see tied to a stake and burned alive."

Seeing as the only fundamentalists liberals seem to like are radical Islamic fundamentalists, it is exclusively Christian fundamentalists that are no good. And this has apparently hurt many Christians' feelings, so much that they have collectively, universally and conspicuously distanced themselves from the term "fundamentalist."

I say poppycock. Racists (or as liberals call them: "Christian fundamentalists") called blacks "niggers" for generations and now blacks are employing the term "nigga" as a badge of brotherhood and solidarity. Why can't Christians do that? Since liberals have denounced, derided and demonized unapologetic Christian fundamentalists like Jerry Falwell, Pat Robertson and John Ashcroft, Christians have begun to see these men as embarrassments. In due course, they have adjusted their form of Christianity so as to have no stomach for the gravity of truth that sometimes emanates from these men's mouths. (While liberals had no problem with what entered Monica's.)

I call these Christians lightweights. There is solid biblical teaching that exonerates, and the realities of American culture substantiate many of the things these crazy cats have said. Furthermore, seeing as how hysterical liberals get over the things they say, Christians should begin taking the hint that perhaps they must be saying the right things. The fact that Jesus enraged the devil by not giving into temptation is not a case for why we should give into temptation so as not to enrage the devil.

When Pat Robertson made the remark on *The 700 Club* that we ought to assassinate Hugo Chavez, liberals reacted as if he had said he wanted to kill Elmo from *Sesame Street* instead of a corrupt dictator allied with terrorist groups. What should *really* embarrass Christians about Robertson is that he later apologized.

In a fundraising letter written in 1992, Robertson proclaimed, "The feminist agenda is not about equal rights for women. It is about a socialist, anti-family political movement that encourages women to leave their husbands, kill their children, practice witchcraft, destroy capitalism, and become lesbians." One feminist was so infuriated with this remark that she decided to set a curse on Robertson by using her recently aborted fetus as a voodoo doll along with the help of her lover, Pam.

Then there is Jerry Falwell, who has indeed said some whacked out things, but at the same time has said some bold and possibly truthful things that he should be commended for, such as when he said in 1991 that, "AIDS is the wrath of a just God against homosexuals. To oppose it would be like an Israelite jumping in the Red Sea to save one of Pharaoh's charioteers." Now hopefully he intended this to be mere speculation as it is no one's business to speak for God but can you imagine George W. Bush having the cojones to say something like that? Unbelievable.

However, when Falwell says things like what he said on September 13, 2001, that "[w]hat we saw on Tuesday, as terrible as it is, could be miniscule if, in fact, God continues to lift the curtain and allow the enemies of America to give us probably what we deserve" (a quote liberals would be praising him for were he not, well, Jerry Falwell), Christians should be discerning. This is not necessarily the quintessence of fundamentalism. You do not have to agree with that statement to be a fundamentalist, even if the statement is true. To be a fundamentalist basically means taking every word of the Bible literally and believing in all of God's miracles, which all Christians should do anyway. This means believing in the parting of the Red Sea, Balaam communicating with a donkey, Jonah surviving being swallowed by a fish, and God having created Dennis Kucinich as a human. (Okay, not that last one.)

When liberals level attacks against "Christian fundamentalists," whether or not you as a Christian consider yourself a fundamentalist, they are talking about you. "Christian fundamentalists" is merely liberals' term for "all Christians." Do you honestly consider George W. Bush to be a fundamentalist? Well liberals do. So why not consider ourselves fundamentalists if they already do? The water's warm. When liberals make that exhausted old comment that "Terrorism is the result of *all* forms of fundamentalism," they mean, "Terrorism is the result of Christian and Jewish fundamentalism which provokes Muslim attacks. It's not the Muslims' fault."

Liberals have blackened the term "fundamentalist" to denote those idiots with no lives who stand outside the funerals of slaughtered homosexuals with "God Hates Gays" signs. To them, those morons (not to mention the Ku Klux Klan) are emblematic of quintessential Christianity, yet the Islamic beasts who attacked us on 9/11 were not really actual Muslims.

It is simply illogical for Christians who believe the Bible front to back to not consider themselves fundamentalists. The use of the term "fundamentals" as it applied to Christianity was popularized by a series of twelve paperback volumes published in Chicago between 1910 and 1915, which were titled *The Fundamentals: A Testimony to the Truth.* This "testimony" declared what were the "Five Fundamentals": 1) inerrancy of the Scriptures, 2) the virgin birth and the deity of Jesus, 3) the doctrine of substitutionary atonement through God's grace and human faith, 4) the bodily resurrection of Jesus, and 5) the authenticity of Christ's miracles. Sounds like everything "moderate" Christians believe, doesn't it?

The intellectual vision behind *The Fundamentals* belonged to Amzi Clarence Dixon, a Southern-born Baptist preacher who made a career out of preaching in Northern Baptist congregations in places like Brooklyn and Chicago. Dixon turned against the brand of Christian modernism that was so pervasive in Chicago—the early nineteenth century's version of "progressive" Christianity—according to which God manifested himself through an immanent presence in nature and history, as opposed to traditional revelation and direct intervention in the affairs of man.

Another champion of early fundamentalism was William Bell Riley, who, like Dixon, was a Southern-born Baptist who preached to Northern congregations. Riley founded the World's Christian Fundamentals Association, which was an organization formed in the interest of combating the liberalism that was bubbling up in what was then contemporary Christianity.

Even back then, there was a problematic disparity between "progressive" or liberal Christianity and what was growing to be called "Christian fundamentalism." Even the fundamentalist Christians around that time period (the early 1900s) were disparaged by Hollywood, just as they are today. William Jennings Bryan, a notable Christian fundamentalist who grew to fame in the heat of the

Scopes Monkey Trial, is portrayed in Stanley Kramer's 1960 film, *Inherit the Wind*, as a raging, sweating, ideological nutcase.

Liberals have done everything in their power to make fundamentalism colossally less appealing to Christians, so as to lure as many of them away from Christianity as possible until Christianity becomes a completely enervated and defenseless religion that they can use to their advantage. That is why it is time for true Christians to reclaim the fundamentalist title, flaunt it shamelessly, parade it around and make liberals even more enraged.

CHAPTER 9

CHRISTIAN PACIFISTS: PRESSING THE "OTHER CHEEK" ON A FIRE GRILL

Far too often, Christians who support the Iraq war find themselves in a debate over the matter with a liberal, and after the liberal has exhausted the whole "Well Bush is like Hitler and you're a Nazi" cliché, he will do something more crafty— he will quote scripture. Now as laughable and ridiculous as the idea of a liberal quoting scripture is, they actually happen to do it a lot. And when you're telling them about the gassing of the Kurds or the assassination attempt on George H.W. Bush or Resolution 1441, they just have to whip out that old used and abused verse from Matthew: "But I tell you, Do not resist an evil person. If someone strikes you on the right cheek, turn to him the other also." This is liberals' favorite verse, although I don't remember any unborn babies slapping any liberals and liberals don't even seem to feel compelled to "turn the other cheek" when it comes to them.

Liberals, being the scriptural scholars that they are, also apply this verse to the death penalty. And more and more, Christians are giving in to their twisted logic. I've heard Christians say, "We shouldn't execute Saddam! We need to take the *higher* road!" Well guess what? Executing Saddam *is* the higher road. They also prattle on about how we need to treat enemy combatants and terrorist suspects like royalty: "We shouldn't do anything to hurt them or torture them, that's not what Jesus would do! We need to take the *higher* road!" Well you know what? Torturing the living hell out of them to the point of unbearable, excruciating pain *is* the high road. Millions of lives depend on it.

There is no doubt that our country became the laughingstock of the Muslim terrorist world when 9/11 conspirator Zacarias Moussaoui was given a sentence of life in prison rather than a death sentence. After he said, "I just wish it would

31

have happened September 12, September 13, September 14," it would have been fitting to stab him in the heart and slit his throat over and over again for each day in September he wished a 9/11 had taken place. If liberals got too squirmy we could've just told them it was a "sharp knife malfunction." So many liberals were saying things like, "Oh, well he *wanted* to die as a martyr, so by killing him we'd be giving him what he wanted." This must mean that liberals actually believe Moussaoui would really be greeted by seventy-two virgins. After all, they are saying that he would indeed "get what he wanted." And they pick on us for the "crazy" things we believe?

Jesus may have been the prince of peace, but he also carried a sword. He didn't turn the other cheek when he came into his father's temple to find it being exploited by money changers and dove sellers (whose ads featured rather unattractive women). He flipped out and went into a furious rage—turning over tables and whipping people. His title of the "prince of peace" implies *inner* peace. But when it came to world peace, Jesus made it very clear that he "did not come to bring peace but a sword" (Matthew 10:34). Liberals paint Jesus as a pushover, and say that because of it, we should be pushovers, and our country should be an international doormat.

Christian pacifists obviously haven't bothered to read the Old Testament. Since the dawn of man, war has been the central agent of the progressive development of world civilization. (Hear that, liberals? "Progressive"! You should love war!) In many instances throughout the Old Testament, God's insistence on wars being carried out almost made it seem as if through war, he was designing the make-up of the world community as he saw fit. War from time to time is a necessity just as filling up your engine with oil from time to time is necessary. Blood has to be shed for life to go on.

Christians should showcase their dignity and self-respect by standing up to flesh-eating tyrants like Saddam Hussein, and their care for the well-being of others by supporting the liberation of what was an oppressed and terrorized nation. In an April 2004 interview, however, (not with *Playboy* this time) Jimmy Carter—who is known as the first evangelical Christian president—was asked about how the "fundamentalist Christian right" has "misrepresented" Christianity, to which he replied, "Well, what do Christians stand for, based exclusively on the words and actions of Jesus Christ? We worship him as a prince of peace. And I think almost all Christians would conclude that whenever there is an inevitable altercation—say, between a husband and a wife, or a father and a child, or within a given community, or between two nations (including our own)—we should make every effort to resolve those differences which arise in life through peaceful means. Therein, we should not resort to war as a way to exalt the president as the commander in chief. A commitment to peace is certainly a Christian principle that even ultraconservatives would endorse, at least by worshipping the prince of peace."

Well I certainly don't recall "peace" being the recurrent "rosebud" of the Bible. From Genesis to Revelation, the theme is what happens to those who follow God (they receive eternal life) and what happens to those who ignore or repudiate God (they get to rot in hell). "Peace" is not a "Christian principle." Forgiveness is. Submission is. Stoicism is—on a circumstantial basis. Jesus denounced vengeance, but he never denounced justice. And justice is not always peaceful. When it comes to Saddam Hussein, when it comes to Osama bin Laden, are liberals going to value peace more, or justice more? Liberals value John Lennon's LSD hallucination of "peace." To the contrary, Christians should value justice, and *inner* peace. After all, Christ never actually *rescinded* the Exodus 21 "eye for an eye, tooth for a tooth" verse. He merely used it as a reference for how it should not apply to vengeance.

In June 2002, a group of Christian theologians and activists, in partnership with the Catholic peace movement Pax Christi, launched an ecumenical declaration on the morality and legality of the war against Iraq. In the declaration they cited Articles 2 and 51 of the U.N. Charter, which stipulate that "the only circumstance under which a sovereign state might invoke the authority to go to war is when an armed attack occurs; and that even in self-defense, it may do so only until the Security Council has taken measures necessary to maintain international peace and security."

One reason as to why Christians should distance themselves from liberalism is the reality of liberals' Manchurian candidate-like submission to the United Nations. Liberals' god (besides themselves and Bill Clinton) is Kofi Annan. Christians' god should remain Christ. A liberal wouldn't swat a mosquito on his arm without full U.N. Security Council approval. They believe that our foreign policy should be directly dictated by the U.N., which was given away by John Kerry's claim during the 2004 election that as president he would try to pass a "global test" before taking any national security measures that might disappoint the French. Liberals don't believe in the sovereignty of America just as they don't believe in the sovereignty of God. That is why they are such fish out of water here. This is a country founded on Christianity and they are inherently opposed to Christianity, so they submit to a godless, corrupt, would-be world government and deny allegiance to the United States flag. And these are Christians talking!

Bizarrely putting Christianity on a par with the United Nations, the declaration further reads: "It is deplorable that the world's most powerful nations continue to regard war and the threat of war as an acceptable instrument of foreign policy, in violation of the ethos of both the United Nations and Christian moral teaching." Christian moral teaching *and* the United Nations? Wow, this must be a really corrupt war!

At exactly what point does "Christian moral teaching" condemn "war" or "the threat of war?" How about I Samuel 15:17-18: "Samuel said, 'Although you were once small in your own eyes, did you not become the head of the tribes of Israel? The Lord anointed you king over Israel. And he sent you on a mission, saying, 'Go and completely *destroy* those wicked people, the Amalekites; make *war* on them until you have wiped them out'''" (emphases mine). Hopefully God appealed to the U.N. Security Council before making that command and made sure it passed a "global test."

"Progressive" Christians let liberals push them around just as liberals let Islamic fanatics push their country around. And they acquiesce to liberals' standards of pacifism and political correctness. They have fallen into the trap of worshiping peace rather than the prince thereof. Liberals advocate the mythological concept of "world peace" but when it comes to creating inner peace they compulsorily dash to their nearest peyote dealer to purchase the requisite supplies.

Christians better put on their armor fast because it's about time to make war on liberalism.

CHAPTER 10

TIME OUT

You may have noticed that I concluded the last chapter by calling for a war on liberalism. And I want to take this time to clarify something very important. You may view me as an extreme right-wing conservative who likes to make enemies out of liberal Democrats. Fine. But truly I tell you, I am not all that interested in the battle between Republicans and Democrats. I am not all that interested in the battle between conservatives and liberals. What I am interested in is the battle between *Christians* and liberal*ism*. You can call me a conservative, but I am first a Christian and am only a "conservative" as an inexorable byproduct of my positions on issues—which you will note, are directly dictated by my inherent Christian nature.

In his book, *Reagan's Children: Taking Back the City on the Hill*, Hans Zeiger writes, "For Reagan's Children, conservatism must be at once more faith based and less election based. At times, the so-called religious Right has appeared guilty of putting politics before Christ. To the eyes of some observers, winning elections seems a more important priority for key Christian leaders than evangelism or discipleship." This is to say, Christianity and conservatism are not the same thing. They may be cooperative, but they are not the same thing. Conservatism is of this world, Christianity is not. The battles we fight over raising or reducing taxes, immigration, even national security, are finite and largely irrelevant in the grandiose context of the universe and eternity. There is a reason Jesus didn't liberate the Jews from Rome. It wasn't his business. Christians must remember that their home is not on earth, but their citizenship is in heaven. We are here on a business trip. On business trips we hold meetings with other business people and try to do business with them, and it's okay to throw the occasional cocktail party after 5 p.m. when the meetings are over, and a drunken fight may break out later into the night. But our concern is not throwing cocktail parties, it is not settling drunken quarrels. It is holding the meetings. And our home back in San Diego is as much our home as is the suite we're currently staying at in Denver. James 4:4 reads, "You adulterous people, don't you know that friendship with the world is hatred toward God? Anyone who chooses to be a friend of the world becomes an enemy of God." In addition, the people we try to do business with may be feisty, obnoxious and may answer to the names Boxer, Reid or Kennedy, but they are not our enemies. Remember, liberals are not the devil. They're just *possessed* by the devil, that's all.

As Christians, we are not called to make enemies out of our fellow humans. It's one thing to have opponents in warfare, or political opponents, but we must always stop to remind ourselves that we all share in the fellowship of man. As Proverbs 25:21-22 reads, "If your enemy is hungry, give him food to eat, if he is thirsty, give him water to drink. In doing this, you will heap burning coals on his head, and the Lord will reward you." What better way to heap burning coals on the heads of liberals than to give them the last word in a squabble laden with ad hominem attacks and vitriol?

That doesn't mean we should stop telling the truth about them. You see, to us, when the Daily Mirror calls us "dumb" for voting for George W. Bush, or when Janeane Garofalo calls the GOP the party of the "dumb and the mean" when there has been no statistical measure of Republicans' collective I.Q., these are obviously taken as vitriolic personal attacks and should be. But when we tell the mere truth about liberals, by saying say, that they have a history of treason when there *has* been material proof of that (just look at their behavior throughout the Cold War up to John Murtha's call for surrender in Iraq in November 2005) they see it as a vitriolic personal attack on them, or scream "McCarthyism!" We shouldn't be discouraged from being frank because of this.

However, I hate to use this cliché but *liberals are people too* and we should not make enemies out of them. I have been accused of being too caustic in some of my columns over the past couple years because, I admit, I went through a long phase of waking up every day with a burning ambition to fight the liberals with all my might because of what they stood for. (And then I got out of bed and had a bagel with cream cheese.)

Forgive me if I have seemed overly caustic in my language throughout this book, as I still struggle with having to contain what is and shouldn't be a bubbling resentment against liberals in general. They are an infuriating bunch, aren't they? But one of the reasons the devil makes them so infuriating by nature to us right-thinking creatures is possibly to lure us into becoming like them—that is to say, to seduce us into the compulsion to take on God's role and pass judgment on mortals. A lot of what I have written thus far has probably stirred a deep ocean of sympathetic rage among you conservatives and Christian conservatives. Good. But channel it correctly. Even the Democrats are sometimes capable of this.

On September 21, 2006, after Venezuelan President Hugo Chavez addressed the U.N. and made the previous speaker, Iranian President Mahmoud Ahmadinejad, look like Mother Teresa, calling President Bush the "devil," and ranting on about how Bush is a drunk who "walks like John Wayne," Rep. Charlie Rangel, one of Bush's fiercest and most redundant, annoying and tireless critics, exclaimed, "You don't come into my country; you don't come into my congressional district and you don't condemn my president." Of course, in his statement, Rangel just *had* to make the trite comment that "it was [also] not helpful when President Bush referred to certain nations as an 'axis of evil.'" (I guess you can't have your cake and eat it too. Liberals still won't get over the idea of an American president recognizing evil overseas—when it actually *is* evil.)

The congressional deer in the headlights from San Francisco who is basically the other most tireless and nit-picky critic of Bush in the House of Representatives, Speaker Nancy Pelosi, (basically to the House what smack-talker Harry Reid is to the Senate) commendably took Bush's side and called Chavez a "thug."

As heated and as passionate as we may be about politics, as Christians we must take time to withdraw from the arena and leave everything up to God's will, and if he calls some of us to be instruments in the service of the administration and realization of that will, so we will be. But God will have his way with the abortion doctors (and it won't be pretty!), he will have his way with obstinate homosexuals, he will have his way with those who simply deny him. Does this mean I am advocating apathy? Certainly not! We can work through the law to make changes in the path America takes. As cathartic as they may be, the bombings of abortion clinics just aren't cutting it. As Romans 13:1-2 reads, "Everyone must submit himself to the governing authorities, for there is no authority except that which God has established. The authorities that exist have been established by God." That's right. Even Hitler, and yes, even the Clintons. Bad things happen according to his will which facilitate good things.

Think about it. Were it not for the exposure of Watergate, the Republicans may never have thought to get their act together. Were it not for the Jimmy Carter presidency, Republicans may not have had the precious time to regroup, reform, and reproduce Ronald Reagan in his element—and without the disastrous nature and pessimism of the Carter presidency, Reagan may not have had something to juxtapose his shining, sunny optimism with (which pretty much won him the 1980 election), as well as the exceptional character he showcased in office which earned him another victory in 1984. Had 9/11 never happened,

America may have remained immersed in the lethargy induced by the Clinton administration and may not have been awoken to the imminent threats of rulers like Saddam Hussein, the Iranian government, and groups like al-Qaeda. (Five terrorist attacks against Americans throughout the Clinton presidency clearly didn't wake us up enough.) Had Howard Dean's *authority* as chairman of the Democratic National Committee not been *established by God,* the Republicans wouldn't be able to boast that their opposing party is led by a raging psychopath.

If your principal cause in life is to fight for less government spending or a stop to illegal immigration, your cause is worldly and your priorities as a Christian are in the wrong place. I do not take up a cause against the ACLU and its war on Christianity in the public square as a Christian, but as a patriot. God will have his way with them. Fighting abortion, terrorism (redundant, I know), corruption in the church and the liberalization of the church and fighting for the freedom of the Iraqis *are* battles worth fighting in the name of Christ. Politics are fun, but we are not called to be politicians, journalists and commentators. We are called to be representatives of Christ; outcasts; strangers to the world. The rest is in God's hands.

In 1999, after several people left an ultra-conservative political party called the Constitution Party (or in California, the American Independent Party) on account of its embrace of Mormonism and pluralism (and some complained that a Jew had been elected vice-chairman), they formed what they called the American Heritage Party. As one member proclaimed, the party "affirms its belief in the triune God of the Holy Bible and acknowledges that the Bible is the highest and final authority to which all other authorities and ideas must ultimately yield." The party's National Chairman, Dan Eby, said in an interview, "We clearly felt that there needs to be a Christian political party because there are the Republicans and the Greens the Libertarians and the Democrats, and the only reason that the Republicans and the Democrats are so big is because they're organized in so many counties—they've been around for a while. But the alternative, of course, is to not have a political party and to just educate. But, what do you do with that? What if somebody wants to run for office? Well, by having a Christian organization in its realm, that actually has as one of its purposes to elect leaders— men into office—that political party allows you to do that. It allows you to function in that way—a national Christian party whose purpose is to elect Christian leaders."

So what the leaders of the American Heritage Party are seeking to do is to implement an "explicitly Christian" government. The problem here is that there is no biblical basis for an explicitly and exclusively Christian government. The

Apostle Paul never talks about how we should implement governments. We need to focus on the church first, the state second. Basically, what the party is advocating is a theocracy; the Taliban only with Christianity and without the violence. Furthermore, it is impossible to receive the support of the American people while making a sweeping denunciation of pluralism. Yes, our country has Christian roots, but it was those Christian roots—that notion that all men are loved by God equally (or "created equal" as Thomas Jefferson put it)—that gives ethnic, religious, and intellectual diversity a place to call home. It is also the basic presupposition adherent to those Christian roots that reminds us that man is inherently evil and therefore in need of governmental supervision, checks and balances, term limits, and the occasional punishment of having to listen to a speech by Al Gore.

In light of this, how is a purely Christian government even feasible, given the corruption of man? The church would be disgraced by any abuse of power on the part of the state—which is always inevitable. And it seems as if by instituting such a government, they would be taking on the role of God. It must be remembered that governments can control how people are taxed, whether or not they are sent to war, and what laws they are to live by—they *cannot* control the culture. II Chronicles 7:14 reads, "[I]f my people, who are called by my name, will humble themselves and pray and seek my face and turn from their wicked ways, then will I hear from heaven and will forgive their sin and will heal their land." Such massive national repentance cannot be contrived by a government. What they are doing is overestimating the power and authority of man to bring about God's will, or at least what they *think* is God's will. The mere quest of seeking Christian power, control and authority is an egregious and liberal concept and is not what we are called to do. For example, Pat Robertson once said, "The mission of the Christian Coalition is simple ... to mobilize Christians—one precinct at a time, one community at a time—until once again we are the head and not the tail, and at the top rather than the bottom of our political system." He went on to predict that "the Christian Coalition will be the most powerful political force in America by the end of this decade," and, "We have enough votes to run this country ... and when the people say, 'We've had enough,' we're going to take over!" Whoa there, cowboy.

Too many Christians have enveloped themselves in this grandiose passion for governance to the point of which they have sought not to make disciples as Christ called us to do, but to build an empire out of Christianity; to use their faith as a weapon in the pursuit of power. Neither Jesus nor Paul gave us any directives regarding governing. What we are called to do is serve, and if we feel called to *publicly* serve, we must do so with the incentives to act as a Christian would—to remember that the power we have is derived from God, but must separate our governance from our discipleship, the latter being far more important. Protecting our home (America) is a noble cause, but it should not be our primary cause. I personally believe that it's the little things we do in God's name that God loves so much. Helping your friend find his car keys; giving him a ride to work if he doesn't find them even if you have a lot of work to do; buying a homeless person lunch even when you're hungry and you only have enough money for one double-double from In-N-Out; telling Dennis Kucinich that he has a chance of being president someday, et cetera. The simple things are what make us stand out as Christians in the way we should stand out—not complaining about Gavin Newsom, Michael Newdow and the ACLU ad nauseam. Those things matter, but as Christians we should not let ourselves get so heated over worldly conflicts. Romans 8:28 reads, "And we know that in all things God works for the good of those who love him, who have been called according to his purpose." The final chapter of this book is called "We Are Losing." We may be losing the battle for America's soul, but the greater battle between good and evil has already been won. Just not in our time zone yet.

CHAPTER 11

CONFRONTING PERSECUTION

The battle against pathetic, disgustingly hideous lawyer clubs like the ACLU should not be fought by us as Christians, but as patriots fighting for the preservation of religious freedom and the restoration of America's Christian heritage. While I may have made a subjective documentary about the secular left's crusade to ban Christianity from the public square on the basis of their fundamental misinterpretation of the Establishment Clause, I did not do it to serve God, but to defend the dignity of Christians in America who are being bullied around, and to serve America itself. It is one thing to serve Christians, it's another thing to serve Christ. It's one thing to serve your country, it's another thing to serve God.

On no account has God explicitly appointed someone like, oh, let's just say me, to liberate the American Christians from social subjugation and to throw the ACLU lawyers into the sea as was done in Moses' liberation of the Jews from Egypt. (Although the idea has gotten me all riled up and antsy now. I'll chew some gum.) He has called us to make disciples and to serve him and serve eachother. I may have called ACLU Executive Director Anthony Romero a man who is "against everything good, pure and holy in life" in one of my columns, but he is not my enemy. His boss, Beelzebub, is.

For years, I have taken up intellectual arms against the ACLU, both in my columns and in my documentary, and I continue to do so. But I don't do it because I feel it is my Christian duty to do so. I do it because they piss me off. Insanely. You have no idea. And people wonder why I suffer insomnia.

I have rallied a lot of support for a movement against the ACLU. I have met with leaders of organizations that combat the ACLU, such as Brad Dacus of the Pacific Justice Institute, and of course, Judge Roy Moore of the Foundation for Moral Law. I believe all Americans who love freedom should unite against this common menace—but it will be a worldly battle.

We should not wage war on the ACLU because they are harming Christians or harming Christianity, but because they are harming America. They are a fascist organization seeking to institute an exclusively secular state by ridding America of any trace of Christianity. Here's where the case for war comes in. America needs Christianity, because without it, there is no public acknowledgement of man's inherent fallibility and subordinance to God. Without that, man *becomes* God, and tyranny is ushered in. In addition, if it is not recognized that our rights are endowed by God, as Thomas Jefferson of all people wrote, then the source of our rights will be the state—and what the state gives the state can take away. (Note to my regular readers: I know I have made this point countless times before. Forgive me for repeating it again.)

We should fend off attacks by the ACLU in the interest of freedom, not in the interest of fulfilling God's will. The ACLU disrupts our religious freedom—it does not disrupt God's will. God's will is for us to suffer. God's will is for us to be persecuted. We all should expect it. Someday we'll be having church gatherings in our basements and there's nothing we can do about it. II Timothy 3:12 reads, "In fact, everyone who wants to live a godly life in Christ Jesus will be perse-cuted." Jesus himself warned of persecution on a grander scale than ACLU law-suits when he said in Matthew 24:8-10, "Then you will be handed over to be persecuted and put to death, and you will be hated by all nations because of me." We may resist it, we may fight back, but we should do so in the name of liberty for America—not in the name of God. As Americans we should resist it, but as Christians we should endure it. I Corinthians 4:12 reads, "When we are cursed, we bless; when we are persecuted, we endure it." God's work is not the extermi-nation of the ACLU as an organization—when the time comes, he will judge those involved accordingly. (And they'll probably whine, "What's your constitu-tional basis for sending us to burn in hell? The Establishment Clause doesn't sup-port what you're doing. And are the Geneva Conventions abided by down there? We demand a civil trial. Can someone get Mark Geragos on the phone?")

Do not think that Judge Roy Moore's battle to keep the Ten Commandments in the Alabama State Judicial Building was fought in vain. Judge Roy Moore is the most admirable public figure in America. I was hanging out with him in his office in Montgomery in December 2005, listening to him talk about his guber-natorial campaign. At one point he said, "If I was told that I could be governor if I just said I wanted to be, I'd say *no*. I have to know it's in God's will." So here is a man who fights the battle for religious freedom in America, but separates his worldly battles from his pursuit of God's heart, not confusing the two. Too many of us are making that confusion—that just because we fight for the Salvation

Army's right to require divulgence of applicants' religions and affirmation of the Army's Christian mission, or for the Boy Scouts' policy of excluding gays in observance of their Christian background, or for the preservation of the words "under God" in the Pledge of Allegiance, or for Nick Lassonde to praise God in his high school salutatorian speech, we are somehow serving God. We don't *need* religious freedom to have a relationship with Christ. At least we shouldn't need it. Millions of Christians in the Roman Empire did without it. Millions of Christians in the Soviet Union did without it. About a dozen Christians in Hollywood do without it. The Apostles did without it—and they led a revolution that saved and is still saving millions of souls up to today.

Nevertheless, religious liberty is something to be pursued out of love for our country and for our fellow believers. But our real priorities should stay with our non-believing friends. It shouldn't matter what happens to us, but what happens in the hearts of those we minister to. I care deeply about the spiritual well-being of all my friends, relatives and colleagues—and the billions of people I don't know. I couldn't care less if I died tomorrow, except that it would be an inconvenience for my friends and family and all you poor souls who would've gotten to read my finished book but didn't get to.

II Timothy 2:2-4 reads, "Endure hardship with us like a good soldier of Christ Jesus. No one serving as a soldier gets involved in civilian affairs—he wants to please his commanding officer." Fighting for religious freedom is a civilian affair. No one needs it. We could use it, but no one needs it. To be a soldier of Christ is to serve others and to make disciples. Fighting abortion is being a soldier of Christ, inasmuch as it involves the serving of others, and with the ACLU's sponsorship of abortion I guess you have *one* of two good reasons to fight the ACLU in the name of God—but religious liberty is not the other. It has been reported that members of the ACLU and other groups including Americans United for Separation of Church and State and the Mainstream Coalition attended services at one point at conservative churches in Kansas and Missouri to "monitor" the sermons regarding moral issues—namely homosexuality. This is where these godless lawyers are *really* doing damage—intimidating the church into watering down Christianity. There's an opportunity for Christians to fight them as true soldiers of Christ—in defense of God's word.

Let's continue to strive to preserve religious liberty in this country for this country's sake. Let us remember, however, that this is a civilian affair and should never take precedence over our acts of ministry.

CHAPTER 12

THE TROUBLE WITH EVANGELICALISM

(Note to readers: The views expressed in this chapter are speculative and should not be taken as objective fact.)

Anyway, let's get to the point. A sixteenth century French Protestant reformer by the name of John Calvin wrote a book called *The Institutes of the Christian Religion,* in which he wrote, "We may add, that each individual is brought under particular influences according to his calling. Many examples of this occur in the Book of Judges, in which the Spirit of the Lord is said to have come upon those whom he called to govern his people, (Judges 6: 34.) In short, in every distinguished act there is a special inspiration. Thus it is said of Saul, that 'there went with him a band of men whose hearts the Lord had touched,' (1 Sam. 10: 26.) And when his inauguration to the kingdom is foretold, Samuel thus addresses him, 'The Spirit of the Lord will come upon thee, and thou shalt prophesy with them, and shalt be turned into another man,' (1 Sam. 10: 6.) This extends to the whole course of government, as it is afterwards said of David, 'The Spirit of the Lord came upon David from that day forward, (1 Sam. 16: 13.) ... And certainly experience shows when those who were most skilful and ingenious stand stupefied, that the minds of men are entirely under the control of God, who rules them every moment. Hence it is said, that 'He poureth contempt upon princes, and causeth them to wander in the wilderness where there is no way,' (Job 12:24; Ps. 107: 40.)"

Most significantly, Calvin also wrote, "While I admit that those who hold that man has no ability in himself to do righteousness, hold what is most necessary to be known for salvation, I think it ought not to be overlooked that we owe it to the special grace of God, whenever, on the one hand, we choose what is for our advantage, and whenever our will inclines in that direction; and on the other, whenever with heart and soul we shun what would otherwise do us harm. And the interference of Divine Providence goes to the extent not only of making events turn out as was foreseen to be expedient, but of giving the wills of men the same direction."

Calvin's constructive criticism of those who sweepingly proposed the theory that man is driven exclusively by his own will exonerated the case for the theory of predestination. The notion was completely categorically antithetical to the more Deistic approaches to theology in that it held a higher appreciation for God's influence on the heart of man. Calvinism assumed the pervasive presence of an awesome, tough-loving God—who made up his mind pretty quickly (hence how it conflicts with the God-as-female theory) about who inherited his kingdom and who was subjected to eternal damnation.

Still with me? Didn't think so. I'll go on anyway. In the 1970s, partially as a reaction against the cultural hedonism and legal secularism that had arisen in the previous decade, a new national Christian movement called "evangelicalism" came into being. Denounced as it was by liberals for being just a resurrection of early twentieth-century fundamentalism but with more media sensationalism, some of the early leaders of the movement did exude a fundamentalist presence— such as Pat Robertson, whose broadcast network, *The 700 Club,* became a particular vanguard of the movement, and Jerry Falwell, who spearheaded the Christian lobbying group, the Moral Majority—the fate of evangelicalism over the course of the four decades that followed took a turn in many ways that was far from fundamentalist. The isolation and rigidity that typically characterizes fundamentalism is inherently contradictory to the idiosyncracies of modern evangelicalism. In fact, fundamentalism today is more incorporative of the Calvinist mentality on account of its aforementioned traits. Evangelicalism puts more emphasis on Christ's final words in Matthew 28:19, "Therefore go and make disciples of all nations," while Calvinism puts its emphasis on Christ's words in Matthew 22:14, "For many are called, but few are chosen."

The problem is, many Calvinists disregard Matthew 28:19 and many evangelicals disregard Matthew 22:14. In 2005, Jael Phelps, the granddaughter of Rev. Fred Phelps Sr., a Bible-thumping ass clown whose modus operandi when it came to spreading the word of Christ's abiding love by picketing the funerals of AIDS victims, ran for the Topeka City Council against lesbian Tiffany Muller on an anti-"dyke" platform. When questioned about the authenticity of her faith in light of such remarks on MSNBC's *Scarborough Country,* the girl replied, "I'm not about savin' any souls. That's the Lord's prerogative." Though in this book I defend fundamentalists, and happen to be one myself, many fundamentalists seem to put so much weight on denouncing, denouncing, denouncing rather than merely representing Christ with humility, with the idea that because of their respective and allegedly respectable lifestyles they are somehow superior to the heathens. Evangelicals have this problem and then they don't. They don't have it in the sense that they tend to acknowledge that every human is "called," and is therefore equally worthy of salvation which clearly compels them to minister on such a grand scale, but they do have that problem in that they are so passionate about saving souls that they feel if a soul isn't saved, the person is a failure.

Now let's get a few things straight here. Christians do not save souls. They don't even come close. They witness and minister, but God works in the heart of the non-believer "to will and to act according to his great purpose." (Philippians 2:13) His purpose may not be for that person to inherit his kingdom, but that doesn't mean his purpose for them is less important than his purpose for those who follow him. Romans 9:21 reads, "Does not the potter have the right to make out of the same lump of clay some pottery for noble purposes and some for common use?" Those who are made for common use are in no way inferior, and their lives are not lived in vain. They fulfill God's will just as much as Christians do. They just don't willfully or cognizantly serve him and maybe God doesn't want them to. It doesn't mean he hates them. Humans who live hedonistic lifestyles have done many things to facilitate God's plan. Remember Rahab, the prostitute who gave shelter to Joshua's spies and lied to the king of Jericho to protect them? God eventually delivered the land of Jericho into the hands of Joshua and Rahab was an indispensable instrument in the process of that outcome.

The character in the Bible besides Christ whom I admire and identify with the most is the Apostle Paul. While I always believed in Christ, for years I lived a lifestyle tremendously contrary to that of a devoted follower of Christ; doing things that were irresponsible, unhealthy, self-destructive, illegal, and deadly. I was the last person anyone would ever expect to be writing a book preaching to Christians about how they should live, think, and act. I was the last person anyone expected to give up what I was doing because I was in so deep. I ended up facing a traumatic experience, picked up the Bible, read the whole thing, read the New Testament over and over and over again—even during class when the teacher wasn't looking, committed suicide to sin, gave everything to Christ, and began witnessing to people, especially one very important person who says I changed her life. When I told people I had given up what I had been doing for so long, they literally thought it was a joke. I have many regrets, especially two—only one of which I will share with you. During high school I had a close friend with whom I hung out every day, doing the things we shouldn't have been doing. He was as messed up as me. He went away for a while, and a few months after my rebirth, he called me. I saw him a couple times after that—once while I was working, once at a party—but I never told him the good news because I didn't think he'd understand. Not long after, he died. It was on account of the things he was doing, that I had been doing at the same level in the past, that he died.

To this day I wonder a few things. First of all, why did God spare me? It very well could have been me who died. Second of all, why did he pick me of all people, out of the blue, to spread the truth about him publicly? What were my credentials? But then of course, while Paul was viciously persecuting Christians out of pure, unprovoked hatred, God randomly said, "Oh, I've got a great idea. I'll use him to be my most influential servant and minister and author epistles that will change billions of lives for millenniums to come. Hey, Saul! Yeah, I'm talking to you! Get over here!" Hello??!! The third thing I wonder (and deeply regret), is why God put this friend in my life if he knew I wasn't going to do what I could to save his life—not only that, but why *didn't* I do what I could to save his life when I had the chance?

Such things compel me to reflect on the overwhelming importance of evangelism—a practice that has been rejected by Calvinists and abused by fundamentalists in how they conduct it in an accusatory, fire-and-brimstone fashion rather than a manner that bears the fruits of the spirit. Of course denouncing the fruits of evil is important, and of course most of my writing focuses on that, but that's not when I'm evangelizing. That's when I'm venting my righteous rage in the interest of not going insane by the internalization thereof. Non-believers aren't going to stop doing what they're doing just because you tell them it's sinful. They'll stop doing it if you tell them the good news and they believe it. *Then* you can be Peter Finch in *Network* and be an angry prophet denouncing the hypocrisies of our times.

My main problem with evangelicalism is how vulnerable it is to abuse. Churches have become so emphatically evangelical that they have instilled in themselves a spirit of desperation and narcissism that has entranced them with a yearning to vacuum up as much attention, membership and visitation as possible with the wrong motives. This has become the case for many megachurches—this standard of measuring the success of the church on the basis of how many people attend it. Before I moved down to Southern California, I was researching and calling churches in Ventura—the town I was moving to—to find out where I was going to go. Only two called back. The first was a Baptist church that seemed refreshingly conservative but once they told me they did street-preaching I said "Um, no." When an elder from the other church, Community Bible Church, called me, he told me that they didn't care if I decided to go to their church or not, they just hoped I found the right one for myself. That was the pitch that got me to go.

It is important that we find a compromise between the Calvinist and the evangelical mentalities. We can't take an armchair approach to the non-believing world, but we can't think that we can convert everybody. If you have a close relative on his deathbed, and he's not a believer, you can graciously read scripture to him and share your testimony with him. But if by the time he passes he doesn't confess with his tongue that Jesus is Lord, respect God's decision. It was God that was in control of his heart, not you. Don't see your deceased relative as a failure, and don't see yourself as a failure. It would be convenient for us all if George W. Bush, John McCain and Ted Kennedy were in control of heaven's immigration policies, but they're not. Most of us will end up stuck in Tijuana for good. But that's where God wants us to be and maybe where he wants to stay, and if God wants us or our loved ones to stay, we should stay with respect for his will. Just don't drink the water.

CHAPTER 13

LIBERALISM: THE DEIFICATION OF MAN

They may not know it, but both fiscal and social conservatives owe a lot of their political philosophies and the disparities they have with their liberal ideological opponents to a seventeenth century English philosopher whom I mentioned earlier in the book named Thomas Hobbes. In his book, *Leviathan,* Hobbes writes of the inherent corrupt nature of man and the consequent need for governmental supervision. He claims that without government, the world would be governed by jungle politics.

In that book, Hobbes writes: "So that in the nature of man, we find three principal causes of quarrel. First, competition; second, diffidence; thirdly, glory.

"The first maketh men invade for gain; the second, for safety; and the third, for reputation. The first use violence to make themselves masters of other men's persons, wives, children and cattle; the second, to defend them; the third, for trifles, as a word, a smile, a different opinion, and any other sign of undervalue, either direct in their persons, or by reflection in their kindred, their friends, their nation, their profession, or their name.

"Hereby it is manifest that during the time men live without a common power to keep them all in awe, they are in that condition which is called war; and such a war, as is of every man against every man. For WAR, consisteth not in battle only, or in the act of fighting, but in a tract of time wherein the will to contend by battle is sufficiently known and therefore the notion of *time*, is to be considered in the nature of war as it is in the nature of weather. For as the nature of foul weather lieth not in a shower or two of rain but in an inclination thereto of many days together; so the nature of war consisteth not in actual fighting, but in the known disposition thereto, during all the time there is no assurance to the contrary. All other time is PEACE."

This notion of an interminable state of war inadvertently declared by the very birth of man and maintained by the perpetuity of his existence on this earth aggressively negates the popular liberal notion of the remote possibility of world peace. If John Lennon were to have read this he would probably have cried wee-wee-wee all the way home to his octopus's garden in the shade. Boo-hoo-goo-joob.

If all the other eggmen were to read this, they would probably point to the last sentence of the excerpt as justification for their wistful dreams that such "PEACE" is possible, notwithstanding the fact that Hobbes believed such peace was not attainable by man given his condition, and that the best we could do is institute strong governments. But of course, liberals would contend that all the "other time," being "PEACE," takes place exclusively under Democratic administrations. Really? Such as the nearly 1,000 U.S. troops killed under President Lyndon Johnson's micromanagement of the Vietnam war? The fifty-two American hostages captured by the Iranians and held for 444 days under the Carter administration? The eighteen Americans killed in Somalia, two of which were humiliatingly dragged through the streets by raging Muslim savages before President Clinton's Chamberlain-esque withdrawal from the region—giving one Osama bin Laden the impression of the "weakness and the frailty and the cowardice of the American soldier"? All this while they believe war is a product of Republican leadership and Israeli military aggression. Nothing else. Liberals believe that man is capable of instituting world peace in the same way that they believe that the implementation and preservation of an Edinic, utopian socialist society is feasible by human standards—this is a narcissistic notion that elevates man above the chaotic jungle he resides in and is doomed to reside in until the expiration of his mortality.

Hobbes' philosophy coincides very strongly with that of America's founding fathers—except they saw it from a Christian point of view, which holds that man is inherently sinful and fallen, and without allegiance to God, man would become a tyrannical beast. One of the framers, Benjamin Franklin, once said, "I have lived, Sir, a long time, and the longer I live, the more convincing proofs I see of this truth—that God governs the affairs of men. And if a sparrow cannot fall to the ground without his notice, is it probable that an empire can rise without his aid?" This quote is a quintessential acknowledgment of man's inferiority to and dependence upon God on account of his fall in the Garden of Eden. These philosophies have resonated in the form of a governmental system which has survived in America to this day—a system that relies on checks and balances and term limits—both implementations made in observance of man's congenital inclination towards despotism and tyranny.

Indeed, though it is arguable that Hobbes was, himself, a Christian, his philosophy was exceptionally cooperative with Christianity. It is my personal belief that absent the pursuit of God's heart, man is motivated by nothing but fear and desire. It is fear that terrorizes man, and it is his natural desires that fuel his animalistic behavior. On the subject of human desire, David wrote in Psalm 73:25, "Whom have I in heaven but you [God]? And earth has nothing I desire besides you." In Mark 4:18-19, Christ says, "Still others, like seed sown among thorns, hear the word; but the worries of this life, the deceitfulness of wealth and the desires for other things come in and choke the word, making it unfruitful." In Romans 8:5, the Apostle Paul writes, "Those who live according to the sinful nature have their minds set on what that nature desires; but those who live in accordance with the Spirit have their minds set on what the Spirit desires." Galatians 5:24 reads, "Those who belong to Christ Jesus have crucified the sinful nature with its passions and desires." James 1:15 says, "Then, after desire has conceived, it gives birth to sin; and sin, when it is full-grown, gives birth to death." Hobbes, when he wrote of the desire of the human heart, proclaimed that, "Our nature is inseparable from desires, and the very word desire—the craving for something not possessed—implies that our present felicity is not complete." This assumes the presence of an insatiable, everpresent vacuum built within the human heart, the sustenance for which is sinful indulgence; therefore those who live their lives in an effort to satiate this vacuum are inexorably driven to destruction, while, taking scripture into account and applying it to Hobbes' theory, thereby producing the following conclusion—a life dedicated to the pursuit of the spiritual sustenance God provides freely to those who repudiate and suppress the desires of their sinful nature, will be an eternal one. For, according to I John 2:17, "The world and its desires pass away, but the man who does the will of God lives forever." For while man is feasting on his desires, the end times will come "like a thief in the night"—thereby unconscionably inconveniencing liberals staying at the Bellagio who already made an advance payment of $400 for an all-nighter with Courtney Lo-, er, some chick.

Hobbes came at the right time, inasmuch as his writings are an unwitting indictment against the hegemonic systems of the governmental institutions throughout Europe during his time and the centuries that would follow—the systems of monarchy and divine right, which I breezed over earlier in the book. Monarchism has a very inconvenient disparity with Hobbes' writing, which is ironic, inasmuch as his philosophy is, as mentioned earlier, so exceptionally cooperative with Christianity—the religion that the monarchs supposedly predicated their system of divine right upon. What the monarchs clearly didn't take into account as they instituted leaders on the quixotic basis of the presupposition that God had directly appointed them to that position, was the inherent, indispensable moral fallibility of man, which if erected to such a towering elevation, would (and did) breed tyranny. Such theocratic institutions have never been successful—at least taking into account the interests of the civilian populations over which they presided. Even the notion of the potential attainment of worldly power—though "apportioned by a deity"—that doesn't go at the expense of the soul of the wielder of that power, is a particularly liberal and humanistic concept which runs contrary to the very nature of Christianity. The notion of "divine right" invokes a man-made construct of God which is both blasphemous and idolatrous. The defenders of monarchism (though there are very few if any today) could point to a verse that is mentioned in this book twice—Romans 13:1—in which Paul writes, "there is no authority except that which God has established. The authorities that exist have been established by God." However, what the monarchs assumed was that God had established their authority because they were especially *favored* by God; that the basis of God's appointment of them to the throne was reverence for and approval of their personal character and credentials. This would clearly not have been the case in light of the tyrannical, despotic abuses of power that have been documented throughout the ages of the monarchs.

When Karl Marx and Friedrich Engels authored *The Communist Manifesto* in 1848, they wrote that "'Communism abolishes eternal truths, it abolishes all religion, and all morality, instead of constituting them on a new basis; it therefore acts in contradiction to all past historical experience.'" Though this movement was, in ways, manifestly a reaction against the religious, totalitarian institutions that had been particularly predominant over the preceding centuries, and while those institutions were hereby denounced as being dangerously contrary to both the philosophy of Hobbes as well as the religion they had supposedly predicated their systems on, this categorically antithetical system would go on to spawn and influence suppressive, tyrannical, totalitarian institutions of its own, such as Joseph Stalin's Soviet Union, Adolf Hitler's Nazi Germany, Mao Tse-Tung's People's Republic of China, Fidel Castro's Cuba, Katie Couric's *Today* show, and not only that, but it was an even further retreat from Hobbes, and, very consciously, a deliberate retreat from Christianity, both factors being, in their own ways, accountable for the massive tyranny and bloodshed that these institutions would facilitate.

In his 1967 book, *Christianity, Communism and Survival!,* David V. Benson writes: "Communism is a religion, if by religion we mean a collective cult which excites the adoration and motivates the actions of a people. If we disregard its atheism for a moment, communism has all the trappings of an organized religion: its messiahs and saints—Marx, Engels and Lenin, with hosts of other figures who wax or wane in popularity as the ruling priests decide; its sacred scriptures—the writings of these men; a band of apostles and prophets—the Communist Party; an elect nation—the Russian (or Chinese) people; a sense of predestined authority—the immutable course of the 'dialectic' working in history; a millennial period of transition—socialism; which leads to the endless state of bliss-pure communism; redemption—through the sacrifice communists must make to free the working masses; bondage-living under capitalism; sin-rejecting communism; conversion—becoming a communist; and above all faith—that complete trust one must have in the truth of communism's holy dogmas."

The distinct conflict Communism has with Hobbes and Christianity is its idealization of a worldly harmony, with which, of course, comes liberals' quixotic presumption that man is inherently good and therefore capable of instituting and preserving such an Edenic utopia. It rejects the Hobbesian and biblical arguments that man is naturally corrupt, and idolatrously puts man on a pedestal above everything; it implies the supremacy of man over the supremacy of God. It is ironic that every state of which the system presupposed the congenital goodness of man has ended in bloodshed with an irrevocable track record of persecution, genocide and oppression. To Hobbes' credit, such institutions have been definitive examples of the animalistic world man without discipline inevitably catalyzes.

One cannot observe Hobbes' theories and not attribute them to Christianity, or argue that his views were not in any way influenced by Christian doctrine. The title of his book, *Leviathan,* is a reference to the Old Testament, (namely Job, Psalms and Isaiah) in which the Leviathan was an invincible crocodile that ruled the animal kingdom. This was an explanation for why man was in need of a strong government, taking into account Hobbes' observations of rebellion and civil war in England. And while Hobbes' theory specifically expressed the need for *governmental* supervision on account of natural human corruption, this theory complements that which expresses the need for *divine* supervision on account of natural human corruption. In this way, *Leviathan* is a poignant validation of Christianity and an unwitting, prophetic indictment of then-future governments which would not recognize man's subordinance to God.

America's founding fathers apparently didn't want to implement such a government, which is why many of them, including Benjamin Franklin, as mentioned earlier, made public acknowledgements of their faith in and dependence upon God. Even Thomas Jefferson wrote in the Declaration of Independence of "the Laws of Nature and of Nature's God," as well as the claim that "all men" are "endowed by their Creator with certain unalienable Rights, that among these are Life, Liberty and the pursuit of Happiness."

Centuries later, in 1954, Congress passed and President Dwight D. Eisenhower signed into law an act that would put the words "under God" in the Pledge of Allegiance (this understandably having been done in observance of the United States' fundamental, defining disparity with the godless Soviet Union, with which we were at war at the time). More recently, Judge Roy Moore, the former Chief Justice of the Alabama State Supreme Court (who was Chief Justice at the time of this) placed a 2 ½-ton granite Ten Commandments monument in the rotunda of the Alabama State Judicial Building. He did this as an acknowledgement of man's dependence on God, whom he declared was the source of our rights and the God "which our nation was founded on." As a result of these things, the ACLU filed a lawsuit against Judge Moore, and Michael Newdow— one of those bitter, whiny little hotheads who believe in nothing and are sore about it and want to take their existential emptiness out on the rest of the country—is currently leading a movement to take the words "under God" out of the Pledge of Allegiance so that his daughter—whom he doesn't have custody over and who actually likes reciting the pledge, by the way—doesn't have to suffer through having to recite the Pledge in school. It's these elements of humanism which negate the tenets of Hobbes and his book *Leviathan*, which, though it implied the importance of strong government and not necessarily the importance of appealing to a deity, criticized the mentality that would later engulf Swiss-born French philosopher Jean Jacques Rousseau, who wrote that man is basically good—the definitive mentality of liberals to this day. In his 1762 book, *The Social Contract*, Rousseau wrote: "Man is born free, and yet we see him everywhere in chains. Those who believe themselves the masters of others cease not to be even greater slaves than the people they govern. How this happens I am ignorant; but, if I am asked what renders it justifiable, I believe it may be in my power to resolve the question.

"If I were only to consider force, and the effects of it, I should say, When a people is constrained to obey, and does obey, it does well; but as soon as it can throw off its yoke, and does throw it off, it does better: for a people may certainly use, for the recovery of their liberty, the same right that was employed to deprive them of it: it was either justifiably recovered or unjustifiably torn from them. But the social order is a sacred right which serves for the basis of all others. Yet this right comes not from nature; it is therefore founded on conventions. The question is, what those conventions are."

In modern times, the disciples of Rousseau have spent their entire godless lives striving to defend man's right to live a sinful life. Guess what? Man doesn't deserve to live at all. So not only do liberals believe that man is entitled to life (and I don't mean this in any constitutional context), but that he is entitled to live that life in a fashion that is inappropriate, tasteless, and indecent. While he may be entitled to life under the U.S. Constitution—he is not entitled to life under God, much less entitled to abuse the life God has given him. Man is a disgusting creature that belongs in the furnaces of hell. What grounds does he have upon which to proclaim that he deserves anything? But liberals believe that man is a noble creature, and their "progressive" Christian pawns may not cognizantly adhere to this belief, but their discomfort with the subject of sin and the need for salvation constitutes an inadvertent subscription to it. This is why liberals defend gay rights—because they believe, as Howard Dean believes, that gays are born the way they are and because of the immutable fact that man is born good, their congenital orientation must be good too.

This unfounded glorification of man also translates into liberals' political views, which, of course, are inclinations towards socialism. But Hobbes' writings prematurely validate our economic system. Like Hobbes, capitalism takes into account the competitive, self-seeking nature of man and accommodates it. Socialism and Communism childishly misunderstand the nature of man, and eccentrically invest in him a blind faith that he can competently maintain a system of contrived generosity, peaceful coexistence, consensus and egalitarianism that is completely devoid of despotism or elitism. In this sense, when it comes to socialism and Communism, liberals are like kids on mushrooms running up to the roof of a building so they can jump off of it and fly. We all know what inevitably happens to them. It's bloody, tragic, horrific, and like something out of a Tom Savini movie.

Hobbes and Rousseau both tapped into an ideological conflict that has burdened man since his existence on earth—a conflict we will probably be dealing with until our collective demise *because* of the fact that we are, irrefutably, a confused and wayward species.

CHAPTER 14

"BABY BOOMER RELIGION"

Over the past few years of my career in political commentary, I've had the privilege of becoming more and more acquainted with a fellow columnist and author of my generation with whom I share many firmly held sentiments. His name is Hans Zeiger and he is the author of *Get Off My Honor: The Assault on the Boy Scouts of America,* as well as his most recent masterpiece, *Reagan's Children: Taking Back the City on the Hill,* in which I was very honored to be mentioned.

Hans and myself share many similarities but there is also one significant difference between us, and it's probably my fault. Hans relishes in that optimistic "Morning in America" spirit catalyzed by the Reagan revolution back in 1980 and believes that the spirit still shepherds our current generation as we move forward through the course of human events. As with me, I am much more cynical, much more pessimistic, much more neurotic, and I guess you could say I can be very bitter. You've probably gathered all this from having read the preceding pages of this book, and you will probably gather it even more when you read the title of the next chapter.

But I don't discredit Hans. He is a man who knows how to back himself up, and his preferred method, it seems, is to refer to statistics. And I won't argue that recent cultural statistics justify hope for America's future. I won't say why because I want you to go out and read his book if you haven't. I just get a bad vibe from our current state of affairs and optimistic conservative radio talk show hosts just aren't doing it for me. Hans does though. He seems to look deeper than Rush and Hannity, and *still* finds hope! When all is said and done though, Hans and I can both agree that we *both* hold high hopes for God's plan. It's just our predictions regarding the potential courses our culture may take during our generation on which we are still debating.

But anyway, I was thinking of providing you with two of Hans's columns to read while I get up and stretch, followed by a subsequent interview with him.

These are very important columns inasmuch as they touch on the very same subject matter that envelopes all the other pages of this book. Hans is a gifted fellow writer and a passionate fellow activist, and I hope you enjoy his work as much as I do. Read away.

Baby Boomer Religion—Where Truth Evolves
June 22, 2006

COLUMBUS, Ohio—It is an exceedingly foreboding day of thunderclouds in Columbus, Ohio, as I sit here in the press gallery of the Episcopal Church House of Bishops. They've just passed an emergency resolution contradicting the decision of the House of Deputies yesterday to reject a moratorium on the ordination of homosexual bishops and the blessings of unions. Had they not intervened, they would likely have been alienated from the international Anglican Communion.

But as one bishop announced to Bishop John David Schofield of the Diocese of San Joaquin across the table before the vote: "That will never hold where I come from. You'd better know better than that, Schofield."

The House of Deputies concurred with the bishops Wednesday in an act that one deputy approximated near the "height of hypocrisy." Most of them made clear that they had absolutely no intention of "living into" their resolution to affirm the international Anglican Communion's Windsor Report by distancing from the decision of the 2003 Episcopal Convention to ordain a homosexual bishop.

They will not "live into" the Windsor Report because they've already made up their mind to "live into" the homosexual movement. "Living into" is the sort of codespeak used at the 75th General Convention of the Episcopal Church.

Here, they dialogued on dialogue, and on diversity, inclusion, gender neutrality, transgender neutrality. It was at the Eucharist this morning that the first female Anglican primate-elect ever declared, "Our mother Jesus gives birth to a new creation. And you and I are His children."

This is what my friend Dr. Peter Toon of the Prayer Book Society of the USA has called the "New Episcopal Religion." We might just as well call it Baby Boomer Religion.

It is the religion of the "holy spirit" that moves in evolution. Reality changes. Truth changes. As Dr. E. Bevan Stanley of the Diocese of Newark told the House of Deputies on Wednesday, "For some 30 years, the Holy Spirit has been guiding this church into the understanding of a new truth that culminated in the actions in 2003."

That was when the Episcopal Church first ordained a homosexual bishop, the Rt. Rev. V. Gene Robinson of the Diocese of New Hampshire. The "holy spirit" made them do it.

The "holy spirit" is a Babel-god of progressivism. It has evolving purposes and plans that move in the putrid breaths of a few Right Reverends. In "intentional" (another buzzword) flight from the truth, they hold a death-grip on the wind.

The convention is a concourse of upper middle-class baby boomers wandering about in a utopian ambit where clerical garb stands for a world of "justice and peace." Indeed, it was "justice and peace" that the convention adopted as the church's first priority. Evangelism was low on the priority list.

The convention is over now, but the salvation of the world will come about in an ongoing process, a dialogue, as they say, that whirls on and on until any sort of purpose or plan is long-forgotten.

Yesterday spoke the doom of the Episcopal Church. By 8 a.m., the Committee on Social and Urban Affairs had already voted unanimously to close down Guantanamo Bay in Cuba, to discharge a resolution that would remove the church from affiliation with a pro-abortion caucus, and to create a 14-hour time minimum for the church's anti-racism training that is mandated for all clergy and deacons. Earlier in the week, the Convention passed a resolution condemning the Bible as an anti-Jewish document.

But that is all rather mild in comparison to what the Episcopalians did about Jesus Christ on Tuesday.

The House of Deputies refused to even consider a resolution that affirmed Jesus Christ as the "only name by which any person may be saved." It also declared Jesus as "the way, the truth, and the life," and renewed commitment to evangelism.

"This type of language was used in 1920s and 1930s to alienate the type of people who were executed. It was called the Holocaust. I understand the intent, but I ask you to allow the discharge to stay," said the Rev. Canon Eugene C. McDowell, a graduate of Yale Divinity School from the Diocese of North Carolina.

I suppose that says it all. The resolution on Jesus as Lord remains in the rejection pile, because the Episcopal Church is not a Christian church. It is a liberal church. And it is dying with its generation.

Spiritual Viagra
May 16, 2004

There seems to be a proliferation of television ads for Viagra, Cialis, and the other mass-market impotence drugs. There are nearly three times as many Google hits for "Viagra" as for "George Bush." Then there is the most frequently deleted spam title from my email box, something about potions that one can order online to restore vitality. I suppose with the market as it is, Bob Dole's crusade against E.D. is moving toward a victorious end. Yet the question remains, what about the vitality of the soul?

It is a question neglected by an age that wants to feel good in the flesh, but has systematically and painstakingly ignored the overwhelming questions about the spirit. The greatest plague of our time is a drastic spiritual impotence that we might say requires a heavy dose of spiritual Viagra.

It seems that the church would be the source of America's strength, but a new survey shows that a smaller proportion of Americans are going to church than ever before.

According to the Barna Group, the number of American adults who do not attend church has doubled from 39 million to 75 million in the past 13 years, despite a 15 percent rise in the American population. While 21 percent of adults never attended church during a six-month period (with the exception of weddings, funerals, Christmas, or Easter) in 1991, 34 percent are un-churched today.

Churches have particularly alienated men. 55 percent of the un-churched are men. And only 38 percent of Americans who consider themselves "born again" are men. 9 million American men use Viagra. Fewer men have joined churches in the past decade combined.

The un-churched are radical individualists. According to the pollster George Barna, they are less likely to vote, contribute financially to non-profit organizations, or become involved in community activities. Nearly 40 percent of the un-churched are single, never-married adults, compared to 26 percent of the general adult population.

The un-churched are also younger, at 38, than the median age of Americans, 43. Combining the Barna information on age and gender, church demographics are seriously lacking in young and middle-aged men. The face of the American church in 2004 is the elderly woman.

The sissification of the American church has been occurring for over a century now. The release of the Barna survey coincided appropriately with my reading of J. Gresham Machen's 1923 landmark treatise Christianity and Liberalism. "The greatest menace to the Christian church today comes not from the enemies outside, but from the enemies within; it comes from the presence within the Church of a type of faith and practice that is anti-Christian to the core," Machen declared.

Liberalism has so infected American churches since Machen wrote that it is now impossible to speak of churches being entirely Christian. Christianity is not dead, and in fact cannot be. Christianity is dependent on grace that transcends the weakness of humanity. But churches, which can be either churches of God or churches of man, have too often chosen the latter course and find themselves dying.

The reason that so few Americans attend church is that so few churches are Christian. Liberal pastors speak much of unity and peace and social justice and harmony and the like. The human condition and the Cross are seldom preached in many churches. And if the claim seems too vague, I will name names (generally speaking): Presbyterian Church USA, United Methodist Church, United Church of Christ, Evangelical Lutheran Church of America, and the Episcopal Church USA, to name a few.

The decline of the American church is reason enough to despair about the future of America.

Yet there are some signs of hope amongst young Christians. I spent last week on the shores of Lake Huron with hundreds of fellow college students at an Intervarsity Christian Fellowship conference. There seems to be a newfound passion and drive amongst young Christians for evangelism and Biblical doctrine, a theme I will further explore in an upcoming column.

Whatever the trends, the key to our national survival is clear: a new generation of American Christians must seek the grace of God for the renewal of America's religious and cultural foundations.

THE INTERVIEW:

Christian Hartsock: In your column "Baby Boomer Religion—Where Truth Evolves," you coin the term "baby boomer religion." Will you explain what you mean by that?

Hans Zeiger: Baby Boomer religion is all about the process, not about the object of our worship. Instead of fearing and loving God, the mainliners and soft evangelicals have taken to a variety of other tasks ranging from fun to un-Christian. Mainline denominations such as Presbyterians, Methodists, Episcopalians, United Church of Christ, and the Evangelical Lutheran Church are determined to ordain women and homosexuals. The Episcopal Church Convention last summer passed a resolution condemning the Bible as an anti-Jewish document, while rejecting a resolution that declared Jesus as the way, the truth, and the life. Soft evangelicals, on the other hand, care most about having a good time, a deep experience, and filling the church with crowds and dollars. Of course, they would never offend anyone, and it's best to "come as you are." Why is our generation fed up with Baby Boomer religion? Because it asks nothing of us, it makes nothing of God, and it only affirms the meaningless that we would seek out religion in the first place to solve.

CH: You note that at the 75th General Convention of the Episcopal Church, the emphasis was on "justice and peace" and not so much on evangelism. Would you say this is a growing problem among churches?

HZ: It is not a growing problem, because the churches that care more for "justice and peace" (ie homosexuality, AIDS, and abortion) are quickly dying out. It seems that they've aborted their children in the name of "justice and peace," and justice is coming swiftly for the mainline denominations.

CH: You seem to touch on a note of optimism when you say that the Episcopal Church is "dying with its generation." Are you optimistic about this prospective fate or do you believe the Church is having a deleterious and burgeoning influence on Christians today?

HZ: It is tragic that the faith of our Founding Fathers, Anglicanism, is in such disrepute today, but it is better that the church of liberalism go down in defeat than that it survive in the guise of Anglicanism.

CH: In "Spiritual Viagra," you mention J. Gresham Machen's 1923 landmark treatise Christianity and Liberalism. "The greatest menace to the Christian church today comes not from the enemies outside, but from the enemies within; it comes from the presence within the Church of a type of faith and practice that is anti-Christian to the core," Machen declared. How would you say this "type of faith and practice" has progressed over the years?

HZ: Liberalism has turned into a pernicious and suicidal brand of relativism. No longer does it merely ask us to reject certain doctrines as being unlikely, it asks us to reject all of truth. Liberals will find that their legacy is short when they are unable to pass it onto our generation. Only principles can be handed down, not relativisms.

CH: You write, "The reason that so few Americans attend church is that so few churches are Christian. Liberal pastors speak much of unity and peace and social justice and harmony and the like. The human condition and the Cross are seldom preached in many churches." Would you say this is a product of the culture that encompasses these churches? If so, how so?

HZ: It is because the Kingdom is not of this world that it is impossible for the world to understand the kingdom. Churches of this world cannot comprehend the ways of the true and universal Church. They become as one with the culture instead of challenging that culture to repent.

CH: How do we preach the brutal truths about Christianity without driving sensitive people away?

HZ: We must point to ourselves as sinners saved by grace. We must point to God as the Lord of our lives. We must stand in the gaps of the culture, through film, higher education, K-12 education, the arts, parenting, the church, the community. We must engage every part of our society for Christ.

CH: What do you think should be done to confront this liberal menace that is threatening Christianity? What topics should be brought up in sermons, where should the emphasis be?

HZ: Sin.

CONCLUSION
We Are Losing

Between the years of 2004 and 2007, conservative media commentators like Rush Limbaugh and Sean Hannity had been sounding the drumbeat of victory. By this they meant victory for either the GOP or the right. If they mean it for the GOP, they were clearly wrong. If they mean it for the right, they were definitely wrong.

Yes, it was evangelicals and "values voters" primarily who gave George W. Bush his second term of office. But was it evangelicals and "values voters" who got what they wanted? No. They got a president playing dodgeball when Barbara Walters asked him if he wanted *Roe v. Wade* overturned. They got a *Playboy*-defending, gay rights-supporting, *Roe*-is-the-"settled-law-of-the-land" Supreme Court appointment, just before Sam Alito, who was only a back-up plan for the supposedly pro-life Harriet Miers, who, in a 1993 speech had spoken of "the ongoing debate ... surrounding the attempt to once again criminalize abortions or to once and for all guarantee the freedom of the individual woman's right to decide for herself whether she will have an abortion." In 2004, they got all this jive talk about banning "gay marriage," but after that what they got was an extended version of the national "Day of Silence" that is instituted in schools by gay rights activists—a national *"Two Years of Silence."* Perhaps having Elton John stay in the White House really reminded Bush of how much he dug that song "Rocket Man."

But then of course all of a sudden right before the 2006 congressional election, "gay marriage" was randomly an issue that concerned Bush again. And still, conservatives around the country were boasting of their success in preserving a congressional majority for twelve years as well as, of course, Bush's second-term election victory. (There seems to be a "twelfth year curse" for Republicans: in 1992, after twelve years of holding the presidency, Clinton came into office, and the Republicans lost Congress in 2006, twelve years after the Gingrich revolution.) But as I write this (in the last couple years of Bush's term), it is highly likely that either conservatives fed up with Bush's immigration policy (as well as the

factors mentioned above) will refuse to vote and the Democrats will win the election, or Bush will be followed by an even more moderate Republican like John
McCain or Rudy Giuliani, which will act as an agent in the progressive liberalization of the Republican Party, and soon enough it be will be less appropriate to
call the GOP the party of Ronald Reagan and more appropriate to call it the
party of Ron Reagan, Jr.

It is quite possible that the devil had used Bush's re-election as a distraction
from the dramatic liberalization of America; a trick to dupe Americans into
believing that the country was safely dominated by Christian conservatism.
When I measure the condition of our nation I don't just look through the halls of
Congress or the White House or the Supreme Court. I look at pop culture; television, music, movies, and the number of leftover issues in a *New York Times*
newspaper stand. The majority of politicians in power may have an "R" next to
their name, but that doesn't distract from the scores of Americans flocking to
watch a portrayal of a cowboy sodomizing another man. (And no, I am not talking about Bush's March 2005 joint conference with Vincente Fox.)

It also doesn't distract from the fact that in Hollywood, a place John Kerry
says is representative of America's values (and in just a little while he'll be right),
celebrated pervert Alfred Kinsey is touted as a hero and a genius and great American patriot Joe McCarthy is condemned as a liar and a scoundrel.

When I measure the condition of our nation I observe the music and pop culture fads that permeate our current era. In the fifties, it was Buddy Holly and
Elvis Presley and a date meant going to a drive-in movie or stopping and strolling
it at the hop-bop-bop-bop. In the sixties things got a little messy. The music was
great but the generation, going back to Chapter 4, was all about feelings; how it
felt to smoke "grass" at a Jimi Hendrix concert; how it *felt* to eat mushrooms and
listen to *Magical Mystery Tour* or rock out to The Strawberry Alarm Clock on
acid. In the seventies, music was at its best, and we had the pleasure of experienc-
ing the disco and soul scenes, which were just plain fun. No social commentary
music, no need to drop acid while listening to The Spinners, although the
cocaine epidemic was growing strong while foreshadowing its imminent massive
attack in the eighties. Physical pleasure was still a hot priority.

Everything changed by 1980. There were 90,000 people showing up to burn
disco records at Chicago's Old Comiskey Park in 1979. A year later, Jimmy
Carter was ousted by Ronald Reagan. Popular music was no longer so much the
sound of lamentation as it had been in the late sixties and early seventies. To the
contrary, singers like Pat Benatar, Kim Wilde, Annie Lennox and Christine
McVie put out "don't-mess-with-me" tough girl songs which exuded an attitude

of power, invincibility, self-determination and solidarity that defined the Reagan revolution. By now the dominant colors were no longer red, yellow and orange; they were power colors—red, blue, and purple. It was either Ronald Reagan or the coke that made Americans feel so powerful (probably both). They had had enough of Jimmy Carter, they had gotten over Watergate, and more and more Americans were growing to be absolutely fed up with abortion. That was the domestic issue of the decade. Ultimately, the music was positive, Americans' attitudes and priorities were positive and we were winning the Cold War—although the Russians managed to have better hairstyles than us at the time.

The nineties ushered in the self-pity generation, which would peak especially in the 2000s. The self-destructive, existential disillusionment embodied by Kurt Cobain would plague teens from Seattle to Des Moines. Then in the late nineties, "emo" would take over. Whiny, self-pitying bands like Papa Roach and A Simple Plan, who glorified suicide and wrote songs about how they were "cursed for eternity" because they accidentally crashed their dad's car into a wall were now somehow cool.

Why is it that everyone is simply so much happier under Republican presidents? In the fifties, under Dwight D. Eisenhower, everyone except James Dean in *Rebel Without a Cause* and Marlon Brando in *The Wild One* seemed happy. No songs about wrist-slitting then; no thirteen-year-olds shooting smack then. And everyone was so patriotic and united against the Soviet Union in the eighties, under Reagan. No kids snorting blow then! Well, scratch that last sentence. At least people were positive. The only kids whining were the punk rockers, but do you remember any punk rock songs on the soundtracks of any John Hughes movies? Didn't think so.

Today we are immersed in a self-pity culture dominated by a style of music that has its roots in the late seventies, but became vastly more popular in the nineties and is now the hegemonic sound of the present day. Now, in the eighties, rap groups like Run DMC and De La Soul were simply fun to listen to, and it was feel-good music. But now contemporary gangsta rappers just whine and prattle on about how *hard* their lives are and how much society owes them and how *hard* it is for a gangsta rapper to get by in life (you know, like how hard it is to wait for the new pool in your second mansion to be installed), that is when they're not delightfully rapping about sweat dripping from their genitalia.

Now I personally listen to and am a fan of some rap, especially when it's by rappers from my hometown, Oakland. (And I am not trying to sound like John Kerry, who, during the 2004 election, flaunted his multicultural side by saying "I'm fascinated by rap and hip-hop.") I particularly enjoy Oakland rap groups like The Luniz, Hieroglyphics and Souls of Mischief. I even listen to Tupac, despite his politically charged and anti-American debut album *2Pacalypse Now*. (Probably an album Kerry would gush over if he actually did like rap.)

What has transpired is a new generation of youth that was taught by its predecessors, the baby-boomers, to question. But now that the baby-boomers have taken power, being questioned is a little inconvenient for them, thus leaving our generation polarized between being cast to the outskirts of society or embittered without just cause, and it reflects vividly in the commercial markets of pop culture. The young are growing groundlessly hateful towards their own country from having listened to Immortal Technique, increasingly sexually deviant from having listened to Lil' Jon and the East Side Boyz (I would also definitely add Too $hort but that would be hypocritical because I own one and have owned several of his CDs—Oakland pride goes a long way—don't tell anyone though), and increasingly hateful towards society and life in general from having listened to Eminem. Rap may be fun to listen to or dance to (although compared to rock and disco dancing it's about as fun as standing and rubbing up against someone—oh wait, that *is* all dancing to rap is), and it should not necessarily be expunged from society. But its burgeoning influence on our culture should be contained somehow, at least before Trent Lott begins exclaiming that he can't get enough of listening to 50 Cent's *Get Rich Or Die Tryin'* album on repeat.

The reason I bring this up is that rap signifies a particular attitude that is increasingly emblematic of American society. Its values are: conformity, sexual promiscuity, drug use, male chauvinism, racism, anti-Americanism, and most of all, one of the three central factors of liberalism which we went over at the beginning of the book—the self. Rappers rap about how they want it all; mansions, big screen TVs, girls with big asses wearing thongs, expensive jewelry, et cetera. Rappers also rap about how unfortunate they are and how much they deserve better than what God has apportioned them—what *victims* they are. Rap has glorified the victim mentality which is largely the cause of poverty and is an infection in our nation's character. The victim mentality is an entitlement mentality which is synonymous with pride—and it is pride that is the theme of this generation.

In December 2006, a gangsta rapper was invited onto *Hannity & Colmes* to be harangued and guilt-tripped by Sean Hannity over the fact that the rapper had featured himself in music videos performing a stunt that involved standing on the hood of a moving vehicle and hurling the weight of a half-dozen or so deaths of idiotic teenyboppers who had chosen to emulate the stunt. Surprisingly, Alan Colmes took Sean's side as Sean milked the poor rapper's inexperienced and inarticulate debating tactics for all they were worth while running *Faces of Death*-style

B-roll of dumb skater kids tumbling off of moving vehicles and splattering blood all over the pavement every time the rapper opened his mouth. Now I do not hold rappers accountable for what bored, unsupervised kids do with their time, just as I don't hold Marilyn Manson or Oliver Stone accountable for the Columbine massacre. My point here is not to denounce the purveyors of pop culture, but the useful idiots who elevate them to such godlike positions of power.

Christians need to not be so comfortable with how things are. They should be enraged. Righteously enraged, for the sake of this country. There are conservative commentators of course, as I mentioned before, who are doing their part to inform the public about the truth about the Democrats, but the only openly Christian people I see who are standing up to the threat of liberalism and how it infects not only our government but our culture are black ministers and fundamentalists. That's it. As for the assault of liberalism on Christianity—not from the outside but from within—I haven't heard a peep.

But with the help of God, we can protect our culture and society from not sliding *too* fast, even though it will eventually and inevitably slide over the edge and a secular police state will be instituted. Nevertheless, we all have a blind love in advance for the generation that will follow us, as it means our children or grandchildren, and should do what we can to prepare them with the wisdom, the intellectual empowerment, and the protection against worldly evil that they need to survive as we pass down to them as an inheritance this abominable mess the baby boomers have created.

We can protect our religion not only from outside forces like the ACLU, but also from the demons within who are itching to rip it to shreds and lead every Christian away from their faith. And we better get started. It is important that we confront the assault of liberalism from within before all of us disappear. Souls depend on it. There's a scene in the film *Pulp Fiction,* when Jules—played by Sam Jackson—a hit man who is deciding to turn his life around after having just witnessed what he claimed was a "miracle" of "divine intervention," tells his partner Vincent—played by John Travolta—about how he wants to "walk the earth" … "like Cain in *Kung Fu*" … "until God puts me where he wants me to be." Vincent responds by saying, "They've got a name for that, Jules. It's called a bum … And that's what you're gonna be, man, you're gonna be a f—-in' bum." Many of us will be called things like that. That is because we are called to be strangers in a strange land; candles in a dark room. Ephesians 5:11 reads, "Have nothing to do with the fruitless deeds of darkness, but rather expose them." On a massive scale, as Christians we can lead a revolution of ministry while exposing the deeds done in the darkness, and the darkness that envelopes the church today.

We can try all we want to win the battle for America's soul but we will lose. All signs point in that direction. We can do what we can by casting our votes for the only party in which we find hope, but mark my words—more and more Mark Foleys will pop up and be exposed, more and more John McCains will sell the party out, more and more Arlen Specters will steer the party down the path to death and destruction that the Democrats have paved, the party will turn its pack on America, and America will fall. So why invest our whole military budget into a losing battle? Do I mean that we should give up on America? Certainly not! I say we give America up to God. Set our hearts and minds on things above and God will fulfill his purpose on earth through us, and his will for this shining city whose candles are running out of wax will be accomplished. But we must focus on him first, and keep in mind that though we strive for worldly freedom and try to see the best in the human spirit, man will lose.

I know that all this pessimistic rhetoric runs contrary to the spirit of optimism that guided Ronald Reagan in the eighties and earned us victory against the evil empire we faced at the time, and you may find it reminiscent of the cynicism that pervaded America from Vietnam and Watergate up through the Carter administration. And I hold Reagan in a higher regard than I've ever held any American leader. I remember staying up to watch prerecorded coverage of his funeral on C-SPAN at two in the morning in a state of emotional paralysis in June 2004 and asking myself, "What now?" I remember Nancy being gently forced away from his coffin as she struggled to caress her palms across it for just a few seconds longer. As the flags descended throughout the country I remember thinking, "Well, George, America is remembering her finest hour. Better not screw this one up."

In my February 2006 column, "Emulating the Gipper"—written during the month of the twentieth anniversary of Reagan's first presidential inauguration—I wrote that what made Reagan so great and so unique was that he understood the nature of the Communist enemy better than anyone except for possibly Joe McCarthy, Whittaker Chambers and Richard Nixon. For that he should be commended. However, his epitaph reads, "I know in my heart that man is good. That what is right will always eventually triumph. And there's purpose and worth to each and every life." What this proves is that while Reagan may have understood the nature of Communism better than any previous president, he didn't understand it on a deep enough level. After Reagan's death, his son, Michael Reagan, wrote that he had "gone to be with his father, Jesus Christ." (All this while his other wonderful son, Pee-Wee—I mean, Ron, Jr., was using his father's funeral as an opportunity to guilt-trip hardworking taxpayers who don't happen to support

the destruction of live human embryos for medical research into funding a proce-
dure that should already be bombarded with plenty of sufficient private funding
considering the "promising potential" that liberals won't shut up about. Interesting how the apple that falls closest to the tree is the adopted one while the other
two apples—Ron and Patti—fell from a redwood tree in some other forest.)

Reagan's religious background remains ambiguous to this day. A good friend
of mine who met Reagan in person back in the sixties described Reagan as
"exquisitely" Christian. Reagan's own son, Michael, who obviously has more
authority on the subject than my friend, clearly feels that his father was a follower
of Christ. But in his autobiography, *An American Life,* Reagan makes recurrent
references to "God," but never to Christ. His marriage to a pagan astrologist gives
off the impression that either his beliefs in God were suspiciously pluralistic or
that he simply hadn't observed the indispensable wisdom expressed in II Corinthians 6:14. ("Do not be yoked together with unbelievers.") There is no docu-
mentation of Reagan having been reborn *after* his marriage to Nancy, thereby
exonerating this union, as Reagan's account of his faith in God as written in his
autobiography traces back to his childhood.

Anyway, while it is preferential to have a Christian as president of the United
States, it is not necessarily an absolute imperative, as those in the American Heritage Party would have us believe. What *is* an imperative is to have a generally
God-fearing president with values cooperative with Christianity, which we know
Reagan was. Even Thomas Jefferson, whose words in the Declaration of Independence regarding God make the case taken up by Christian activists against secu-
larists, had a dubious religious background. Nevertheless, Jefferson made a fitting
president because he understood the necessity of declaring and recognizing subordinance to the Almighty so as to fend off the prospects of either secular or theocratic tyranny. Ironically, it is also Jefferson's own words—in that 1802 letter to
the Danbury Baptists in Connecticut with the origin of the "separation of church
and state" phrase—that have fueled the secularist movement to this day. Amus-
ingly, Jefferson probably had no idea how much of a perpetual influence he
would have on both sides of the aisle for centuries to come. If he were resurrected
today to discover the apocalyptic clash of ideologies he had instigated, he would
probably take a few steps back and say, "Uh … I didn't say sh—."

I hope you don't think I'm trying to denigrate Reagan's legacy. He was possibly the greatest leader our nation has ever had or will ever have. He believed in
God, he accomplished freedom in the world in the name of God, his values com-
plemented God's (decency, integrity, charity, honesty, prudence, discernment,
servitude), and he probably made God very proud. But, in observance of his epi-

taph, he clearly had a misinterpretation of the nature of humanity as God had created it up until his death (well, to be fair, up until his struggle with Alzheimer's), and this is a humanistic misinterpretation that reflects the humanism that has been both deliberately and inadvertently adopted by churches across America (and across the world); this quixotic reverence for man that has no biblical foundation and that plays into the hands of Satan, who has sought to motivate a quest for God's throne in the human spirit since he appeared as a serpent to that gullible blonde, Eve.

After the Apostle Paul's rebirth and during his subsequent ministry to the nations, as we all know, he authored a series of epistles to churches throughout the world. He wrote to churches like the church in Corinth—a city wrought with corruption, hedonism and the worship of money, Galatia—a city populated with Jews who took overt pride in their preservation of worldly legalism (Jews Paul could identify with given his devotion to Jewish law that incited his hatred for Christianity prior to his rebirth), and Colosse—a city seduced by cultism and paganism. Though I am no apostle, this book is my epistle to the churches of America, which are struggling with the same things the aforementioned churches struggled with two millennia ago—a love for money, which is especially exhibited by sensationalistic megachurches and regular churches which insatiably devour money and irresponsibly pour it into pointless things like rebuilding the sanctuary, repainting the church exterior, enhancing the acoustics in the sanctuary and turning the sanctuary into an amphitheater rather than important things like fundraising for missions trips; questionable interpretations of scripture, which is exhibited by all these "progressive" churches which use the Bible as a manifesto of political correctness without any regard for the contexts and realities of what's written in it; and idolatry, which is exhibited by those same "progressive" churches which put man on a pedestal and cater to the humanist values of "diversity" and "tolerance" and "community." This may not sound like traditional idolatry but that is one of the church's biggest problems—the idolization of man, which is *exactly* what is written on the heart of liberalism.

As I said earlier, we can fight all the worldly battles we want. But man will lose. We are like goldfish in a fish tank—no matter how many specks of food we're fed, we will all end up on the water's surface with our bellies facing up sooner than we expect. We are "a mist that appears for a little while and then vanishes." (James 4:14) Why spend that while on the slot machines? If you have seen Marty Scorsese's film, *Casino,* you may recall when Robert De Niro's character, Sam Rothstein, the manager of the Tangier's Hotel & Casino, fires an employee for allowing there to be three jackpots in one night. A wise casino manager makes sure there are *no* jackpots, ever. The world is a casino and Satan is a wise manager. He wants to keep us gambling, and he wants to keep us losing. And we will lose as long as we play his slots. Before we make a dime, we vanish. In fact by the time we vanish, we've already lost sixty grand.

The modern-day church bears striking resemblance to what the Apostle John witnessed in his apocalyptic visions, particularly in his account of Christ's words as he addressed the 7 churches.

"I know your deeds, that you are neither cold nor hot. I wish you were either one or the other! So, because you are lukewarm—neither hot nor cold—I am about to spit you out of my mouth." (Rev. 3:15-16)

"This vision disturbingly and uncannily foreshadows the inexorable direction the "progressive" church is unyieldingly cruising down.

Being that the "progressive" Christian movement so obstinately insists upon predicating its increasingly relativistic platform on theological penumbras in a desperate attempt to fabricate some McCainian compromise between the humanistic standards of this world and the divine standards of biblical doctrine;

… being that "progressive" evangelicals are allowing themselves to become more and more inured to the "Who's to say?" arguments of post-modern politically correct culture …

… which trace all the way back to the words uttered by the morning star in Genesis 3 as a diabolical cosmic prank to anchor the creation into the bondage of sin …

… by capitalizing on fallible man's preternatural, instinctual inclination towards being "like God"; …

… being that the church itself has so pussilanimously put itself at the mercy of the liberal movement, thereby replacing fear of God with fear of the ACLU, the Supreme Court, and the sensitivities of the PC police, …

… hopefully they won't take personal offense when the Christ comes back to, in fact, spit them out of his mouth.

As it attempts to prepare a spotless bridal gown in light of the ceremony that is about to begin at any second, the church has decided to use its own homemade brands of laundry detergent to blot out stains which could otherwise be blotted out by the blood of the groom.

"As iron sharpens iron, so a man sharpens a man." (Prov. 27:10)

We ought to pray that the yes of our brothers and sisters in the forever family will be opened, and that their hearts will be humbled …

… so that by the "sword of the Spirit, which is the Word" (Ephesians 6:17) … we might be more willing to sharpen eachother in fellowship …

… even at the expense of offending the establishment. You may say I'm a dreamer, but I'm not the only one.

978-0-595-42271-5
0-595-42271-3

Printed in the United States
93575LV00005B/193-195/A